TERMS OF ENGAGEMENT

CLARK M. NEILY III

Terms of Engagement

How Our Courts Should Enforce
the Constitution's Promise
of Limited Government

Encounter Books New York • London

© 2013 by Clark M. Neily III

First American edition published in 2013 by Encounter Books,
an activity of Encounter for Culture and Education, Inc.,
a nonprofit, tax exempt corporation.
Encounter Books website address: www.encounterbooks.com

Manufactured in the United States and printed on
acid-free paper. The paper used in this publication meets
the minimum requirements of ANSI/NISO Z39.48 1992
(R 1997) (Permanence of Paper).

FIRST AMERICAN EDITION

LIBRARY OF CONGRESS CATALOGING-IN-PUBLICATION DATA

Neily, Clark
Terms of engagement: how our courts should enforce the constitution's
promise of limited government/Clark M. Neily III.
pages cm
Includes bibliographical references and index.
ISBN 978-1-59403-696-5 (hardcover: alk. paper)—ISBN 978-1-59403-697-2
(ebook) 1. Political questions and judicial power—United States. I. Title.
KF5130.N45 2013
342.73'041—dc23

2013021210

To Nicki

Contents

Foreword

Judges matter.

Every litigator knows the moment: hearing the crack of the bailiff's gavel, followed by a solemn voice commanding, "All rise." When the judge enters the hushed courtroom to begin a trial or summary judgment argument, the litigators are prepared to marshal their evidence to make the strongest case for their clients. Every detail has been scrutinized and organized, all relevant case law thoroughly mastered. From that opening moment, an effective advocate applies the law to the facts in order to offer persuasive reasons to rule in his client's favor. In many instances, the case will be presented to the judge alone; there will be no jury. The judge weighs the evidence, applies the law, and then issues an opinion. At every stage of a case, through any appeals, judges will play the decisive role in dispensing justice.

Being a judge is hard work and losing parties will always be unhappy, so judges have a real stake in maintaining a reputation for fairness. The respect with which judges and their decisions are received depends on the integrity of those decisions. That integrity rests on their impartiality. Judges are expected to be neutral arbiters who bring wisdom and experience to their task. These attributes need to be consistently applied because every case must be examined on its own merits. The responsibility of weighing evidence and evaluating arguments demands that judges refrain from injecting their personal biases or political beliefs into a case.

But what happens if judges operate under a system in which one side enjoys a practically irrebuttable presumption of legitimacy, so that judges take themselves out of the business of evaluating evidence and consistently rule in favor of that one side? And what does it mean if that presumption doesn't just affect run-of-the-mill cases, but provides the government with a decisive advantage in cases that determine the constitutional rights of all Americans? Indeed, what if judges abdicate their responsibilities and routinely rubber-stamp government actions without regard to the facts or the constitutional provisions designed to limit government?

These are not hypothetical questions. To the contrary, they are questions that go to the heart of constitutional law today.

This book, by a seasoned constitutional litigator, answers these questions and makes a passionate and intellectually compelling case for an engaged judiciary. As an Institute for Justice senior attorney, Clark Neily has represented clients nationwide whose rights have been violated by national, state, or local governments. He has seen firsthand how often the dreams and aspirations of honest, hardworking people are crushed by government when courts abdicate their responsibilities and defer blindly to legislative or executive acts. You will meet some of these IJ clients in the coming pages. Their courage inspires all of us at the Institute for Justice.

There are, of course, defenders of the legal status quo. Apologists for judicial deference claim that the political process is best suited for addressing concerns about government actions. But paeans to democracy notwithstanding, government actions are not entitled to deference simply because they result from a political process involving elected representatives. To the contrary, the Framers were deeply concerned about the dangers of interest-group politics and overreaching government. The structure of the Constitution rejects blind deference to the other branches. The courts' job is to block constitutionally forbidden political impulses, not ratify them under the banner of majoritarian democracy.

The philosophy of deference has led to the judiciary's abdication of its essential role in our system of checks and balances so carefully designed by the Framers. As Neily discusses, what began with expedient Supreme Court decisions to legitimize the New Deal has now been institutionalized by both liberals and conservatives. Along the way, provisions of the Constitution intended to limit government power have been stripped of effect, and constitutional protections for individual rights have been severely eroded. Indeed, for such key provisions of the Constitution as the commerce clause, due process clause, takings clause, contract clause, general welfare clause, and privileges or immunities clause, to the extent there is debate today, it's whether these provisions impose any limit at all on government power. The result is that our liberties are increasingly dependent on the self-restraint of politicians and government officials.

It's no coincidence that the need for constitutional limits on government power has never been more urgent. A philosophy of judging deemed appropriate seventy years ago brought us to this precipice. That philosophy was never a sound idea, but it is woefully inappropriate and unsuited for the challenges our nation now faces.

This book issues a clarion call for what we need instead: judicial engagement. Courts must fulfill their role as enforcers of the Constitution. They must be the "bulwarks of liberty" envisioned by Madison. They must, as Hamilton wrote, keep the Congress within the limits assigned by the Constitution. When the legislative and executive branches exceed their limited and enumerated powers, the judiciary must strike these acts down.

Since its founding in 1991, the Institute for Justice has argued for a more engaged judiciary. We have won major cases and learned hard lessons along the way. And we know how far we must yet go. This book reflects wisdom and insights that come from that experience. It presents a well-developed constitutional theory and intellectually rigorous defense of liberty. If there is one overriding insight, it's that we must never lose sight of the stakes.

People like the IJ clients featured in this book and so many others seek the chance to live as free and responsible members of civil society. Theirs are the aspirations that can and should define our nation's future. But until the judiciary engages, those aspirations will remain at the mercy of increasingly unaccountable government.

—*Chip Mellor*
President and Co-Founder, Institute for Justice

Introduction

Sandy Meadows was a widow who lived by herself in Baton Rouge and loved working with flowers. She had little education and nothing in the bank when her husband died. She'd never had to support herself before, and her only vocational skill was making floral arrangements. Unfortunately, Louisiana is the one state in the country that licenses florists, just like doctors or lawyers.

Sandy tried five times to pass the licensing exam, but it was too subjective. Besides taking a written test, applicants had to make four floral arrangements in four hours. A panel of working florists would grade the arrangements and decide whether the applicant was good enough to set up shop and compete with them. Usually they said no.

When agents of the Louisiana Horticulture Commission found out that Sandy was managing the floral department of an Albertsons grocery store without a license, they threatened to shut it down. The store had no choice but to let her go and hire a state-licensed florist instead. Prevented by government from doing the only work she knew, Sandy had no way to make a living. She had no car, no phone, and, on the last day I saw her alive, no electricity because she couldn't afford to pay her utility bill. In October 2004, Sandy Meadows died alone and in poverty because the State of Louisiana wouldn't allow her to

work in a perfectly harmless occupation—and I couldn't persuade a
federal judge to protect her right to do so.

That's outrageous. It's unjust. And it's unconstitutional. This book
is about the system that allowed it to happen—that led a federal judge
to do nothing to protect an impoverished widow's constitutional right
to earn a living. It's about countless other abuses of government power
ratified by our courts even though the Constitution was designed to
prevent them. It's about what brought us to this point and how we can
begin to fix the problem with something called "judicial engagement."[1]

Judicial engagement means deciding cases on the basis of actual
facts, without bent or bias in favor of government. It means ensuring
that the government has a valid reason for restricting people's freedom
and that it exercises that power with at least a modicum of care. It
means not turning a blind eye when government pursues constitutionally illegitimate ends, such as promoting the anticompetitive interests
of the Louisiana State Florists' Association. In short, judicial engagement means *real* judging in all constitutional cases.

That might not sound like much to ask for, but it would actually
be a radical change from the way things are done in courtrooms
today. And it's the key to restoring constitutionally limited government. Proper judicial engagement would create a level playing field
for people seeking to vindicate their constitutional rights in court. It
would result in a smaller federal government, fewer regulations, and
more room for individuals to live their lives as they see fit. And it would
ensure that when public officials restrict our freedom, they do so on
the basis of reason, not will.

The Founders gave us a government of finite powers and a Constitution designed to "secure the Blessings of Liberty." But they knew
that politicians and bureaucrats could not be counted on to obey those
limits voluntarily, so they also gave us an independent judiciary to serve
as an "impenetrable bulwark against every assumption of power in
the legislative or executive."[2] Unfortunately, our courts are not fully
performing that duty. They are not acting as neutral arbiters in all

cases. They often rationalize government action instead of judging it. As a consequence, we have less freedom and more government than we were meant to have.

In most areas of life today—from how we earn a living, to what we eat and drink, to the homes we live in, to how we care for ourselves when we're sick—we are subject to the arbitrary will of public officials unchecked by any serious effort to enforce constitutional limits on the power of government. It is increasingly clear to many Americans that the balance between individual liberty and government power has gotten seriously out of whack. Most people think government has grown too big and too meddlesome, and that it tries to do too many things that should be left to individuals and businesses.[3] Did we really trade British tyranny for the tyranny of petty bureaucrats like the Louisiana flower police?

Not if the Constitution were being properly enforced. But as Sandy Meadows learned when she challenged Louisiana's florist licensing law in court, all too often it is not. Thus, while the Supreme Court has recognized the constitutional right to earn an honest living for more than a century, that right has become so watered down by decades of sophistry and neglect that it is practically meaningless today. The same is true of countless other constitutional limits on government power. Courts simply refuse to enforce them in any meaningful way, deferring instead to public officials at the expense of individual liberty. The term for that practice is "judicial abdication," and it is why we have far more government at every level today than the Constitution permits.[4]

The opposite of judicial abdication is judicial engagement. In substance, the idea is quite modest: it means consistent, conscientious judging in all cases. Regrettably, courts have strayed so far from this norm that the practical effects of a fully engaged judiciary would be dramatic. Government would shrink considerably if it were required to give an honest account of its actions in court and restricted to pursuing genuinely public-spirited ends when making policy. That's what the Constitution requires as a bare minimum, but judges often do not hold government even to that modest baseline.

This book is not about constitutional theory; it's about constitutional reality as experienced by ordinary people trying to live their lives free from unwarranted government interference. It's about what happens when a bureaucrat in North Carolina prints out pages from a diabetic blogger's website and goes through them with a red pen, telling him what he may and may not say about managing diabetes with a "Paleo" diet.[5] It's about whether the City of Nashville, Tennessee, can make the owner of a car service charge his customers $45 for a ride to the airport when he wants to charge them only $25.[6] It's about whether Florida can make citizens wade through an ocean of red tape and fill out countless forms before teaming up to challenge a ballot initiative.[7]

Those are the kinds of cases my colleagues and I litigate at the Institute for Justice. During my thirteen years as a public interest lawyer, I've tried cases and argued appeals in dozens of courts across the country. I helped design and litigate *District of Columbia v. Heller*, the case in which the Supreme Court held for the first time that the Second Amendment protects an individual right to own a gun. I regularly discuss and debate constitutional issues at law schools from coast to coast, and I receive a steady stream of emails and phone calls from people across the country trying to fend off high-handed bureaucrats and nanny-state politicians who think they know best.

The most significant thing I've learned from these experiences is that there are two kinds of judging in constitutional cases: real and make-believe. The Supreme Court and lower courts use real judging for constitutional rights the Supreme Court considers important, and make-believe judging for rights it doesn't. As a result, you get genuine judicial review in some cases and an empty charade in others. Here's what I mean by that.

I love coconut water. It's refreshing, all-natural, and it makes me think of being on a tropical beach with my toes in the sand. Now imagine two different laws involving coconut water: one law forbids advertising it; the other forbids selling it at all. The stated reason for both laws is that coconut water is unhealthy, and the government wants to discourage people from drinking it.

If the advertising ban were challenged in court, the government would have to prove that coconut water was in fact unhealthy. It would also have to show that some less restrictive approach, such as a warning label, would not be an effective means of protecting people. Suspicious exceptions—such as exempting certain brands of coconut water from the advertising ban—would tend to undercut the law, as would evidence that disgruntled competitors lobbied for the advertising ban and reaped substantial competitive advantages from it. In short, courts would make a genuine effort to determine whether the government was actually trying to protect the public welfare or rather the market share of competing companies.

If the sales ban were challenged, however, it would be a completely different story. There would be no effort to determine the veracity of the government's health claims, nor would it matter if those claims were merely a pretext for suppressing competition. That's because the Supreme Court considers commercial *activity* to be a much less important right than commercial *speech*. Thus, in defending the sales ban, the government would not have to prove that coconut water was actually unhealthy; it would not matter if there were less restrictive alternatives available; suspicious exceptions and exemptions would be ignored; and the legislature's true purpose in passing the law would be irrelevant. As long as the assertion that coconut water might be unhealthy was not technically insane (and coconut allergies, while rare, do exist), then the law would be upheld. That's what passes for judging in cases involving economic activity and other constitutional rights the Supreme Court has deemed "nonfundamental."

The most glaring example of make-believe judging is called the rational basis test. It has become the default standard for deciding constitutional cases, and it is the very antithesis of judicial engagement.

But there are many other forms of judicial abdication as well, such as rewriting unconstitutional laws to avoid striking them down, treating express constitutional limits on government power as rhetorical fluff, and credulously accepting implausible explanations for government conduct. It all boils down to one key point: in some cases, judges make a serious effort to ensure that the government is obeying the Constitution; in others, they do not.

This book aims to show, first, that this is really happening; second, that it is wrong; and third, that there is a better way for courts to do constitutional law. The need for a properly engaged judiciary becomes more apparent every day. We are drowning in a sea of unconstitutional regulations that compel obedience, stifle innovation, and punish morally blameless conduct. We have the highest incarceration rate of any country in the world, and there are so many laws so broadly written that ordinary people commit felonies every day without realizing it.[8]

Besides criminalizing conduct that is neither wrongful nor within the scope of its constitutionally authorized powers, the federal government collects vast amounts of information about individuals to make sure they are following the rules and paying their share of taxes to keep the behemoth fed. The tax code is a disgrace, with hardly any semblance of reason or fairness—a mind-numbing labyrinth of incomprehensible formulas, hidden loopholes, and corporate cronyism that spans more than seventy thousand pages and gobbles up 7.6 *billion* hours a year in compliance efforts.[9] Heedless of the constitutional limits on its own power and indulged by a quiescent judiciary, the federal government now spends 24 percent of our gross domestic product, the highest proportion since World War II.[10] And because government is so much better at spending money than raising it, an increasingly large portion of that money is borrowed from future generations. That is not only deeply immoral, it is a threat to America as we know it. We are, as the writer Mark Steyn likes to say, "the Brokest Nation in History."

How broke? The national debt is more than $16 trillion, an amount so inconceivably huge that it can only be conveyed with illustrations that are themselves scarcely conceivable, like the weight of $16 trillion worth of hundred-dollar bills (17,636,976 tons—about 117,000 blue whales) or how many times those bills laid end to end would stretch to the moon and back (about thirty-five).[11] To appreciate just how deep in a hole that puts us, think of America as an average household with a median income of $50,000. Even without including the unfunded obligations for Social Security, Medicaid, and Medicare, that household would have $320,000 in outstanding loans. Add in those unfunded liabilities and the household would be $1.6 million in debt.[12] It takes real chutzpah to behave so irresponsibly and then accuse the courts of not giving you enough room to operate. But many politicians do precisely that.

In 2013, a series of scandals involving the Internal Revenue Service, the National Security Agency, the Department of Justice, the Department of Agriculture, and other federal agencies reminded Americans about the hazards of free-wheeling government. Everywhere we turn it seems the government is digging its hand deeper into our pockets, putting its nose further into our business, and looking over our shoulders at more things that used to be private. It has red-light cameras, speeding cameras, dashboard cameras, surveillance cameras, cell-phone tracking, email snooping, data mining, and information-gathering programs so secret we'll probably never know about them. It's safe to say that unless you are being very careful indeed, the government has a pretty good idea—or can easily find out—where you are, whom you're talking to, how you're making money, and what you're spending it on.

And in light of the Supreme Court's decision upholding the Patient Protection and Affordable Care Act, commonly known as "Obamacare," Congress can even tell people how to spend their money by penalizing those who refuse to buy things it thinks they should have, like government-approved health insurance. Congress has no legitimate power to do that, which is why the Supreme Court had to pretend the penalty was actually a tax. The takeaway is that if you put enough creative people together from all three branches with the common goal of justifying the government's actions, they'll generally succeed.

And that's a problem, because the primary impulse of government is to regulate. In *Democracy in America*, Alexis de Tocqueville described how government "covers the surface of society with a network of small complicated rules" that "even the most original and energetic characters cannot penetrate." Consequently, he warned, "the will of man is not shattered, but softened, bent, guided" until "each nation is reduced to nothing better than a flock of timid and industrious animals, of which the government is the shepherd."

Speaking of animals, consider what's happening to the Hemingway Home and Museum in Key West, Florida, where descendants of the author's famous six-toed cat Snowball freely roam the grounds. Acting on a tip in 2003, the U.S. Department of Agriculture opened a two-year investigation of the museum and concluded that its outdoor cat accommodations were not up to the department's exacting standards. The museum filed suit, arguing that the federal government had no business meddling with its free-range felines. But in December 2012, an appeals court disagreed, ruling that even though the cats had never been bought or sold and were in fact marooned on an island at the very southern tip of Florida, they were nevertheless subject to federal control because they "substantially affect[ed] interstate commerce." How so? Because the museum featured them on its website and sold cat-related merchandise in its gift shop. Seriously.[13]

The Constitution was meant to protect us from this kind of pettifogging nonsense and keep government on a much shorter leash. So what happened? Judicial abdication, that's what: the deliberate failure to exercise real judgment in vast areas of constitutional law. Our system of checks and balances has broken down because judges so often bend over backward to avoid saying "no" to government. But "no" can be a wonderful thing to say to government. The Constitution does it all the time.

May the government arrest you without telling you why? No.[14] Can prosecutors make you testify against yourself in court? No.[15] May government censor speech, silence critics, or shut down newspapers or websites that challenge its authority? No, no, and no.[16] May it prevent people from voting because of their race or gender? Not anymore.[17] Nor may the government ban guns,[18] abolish jury trials,[19] or prevent the free exercise of religion[20]—things that governments have done routinely in other countries and many still do today.

Those are some of the more explicit ways the Constitution says no to government, but there are plenty of others. Besides dividing power among different levels and branches of government and placing various speed bumps in the lawmaking process, the Constitution restricts government in two basic ways. First, it puts a fence around government and allows it to act only within that enclosed space. The fenced-in area represents the legitimate powers of government, and they are limited. Second, the Constitution surrounds each person with a suit of armor that the government may not penetrate. That armor is made up of individual rights. In protecting the full measure of freedom to which every American is entitled, it is the courts' job to ensure that the government exercises only those powers authorized by the Constitution and that it does so without violating constitutionally protected rights. A major reason why government has gotten so big and so unaccountable is that courts are frequently failing to do that job.

It is difficult to say what accounts for this abdication, but several factors seem to be at work. Among the most basic problems is the misconception of America as a fundamentally majoritarian nation in which the ability to impose one's will on others through law is a sacred right that courts should take great pains not to impede. A related error is the belief that courts should strike down only those government actions that the Constitution unambiguously prohibits—as if the Constitution were merely a list of bullet points with no underlying principles or values. In this view, anything you might want to do—whether starting your own business, raising your own children, or using experimental drugs to fight cancer—must be explicitly protected by the Constitution or else there is no judicially enforceable right to do it. Exacerbating the twin myths of majoritarianism and the bullet-point Constitution is a remarkable naïveté on the part of some judges about the political process and the true purposes for which many laws are enacted. Whether real or feigned, that naïveté manifests itself in a willingness to credit patently disingenuous explanations for government regulation.

Judicial abdication is also fostered by loose charges of "activism" from people who favor a more passive judiciary. As explained in Chapter 7, judicial activism is a slippery term that can be very difficult to pin down. It is typically used to disparage a court decision the speaker dislikes, but without explanation or analysis. In principle, judicial activism cuts both ways regarding government power: that is, a decision improperly empowering government (by upholding the use of eminent domain in *Kelo v. City of New London*, for example) is every bit as "activist" as a decision improperly disempowering government (as many believe the courts have done with respect to abortion). And though one could describe as a kind of "activism" the Supreme Court's persistent failure to enforce the Constitution, I prefer "abdication" because it is more precise and carries less baggage. In legal and policy circles, "judicial activism" is most commonly used to criticize courts for imposing supposedly nonexistent limits on government power. People who accuse the courts of activism in that sense typically call for greater "judicial restraint," "deference," and "humility," which really means a strong aversion to enforcing constitutional limits on government power and an extremely narrow conception of what those limits are.

Some judges may well engage in activism by substituting their own policy preferences for validly enacted laws or the written Constitution, but that problem has been overstated and overhyped in comparison with the much more serious problem of judicial abdication. Drumbeat charges of activism have helped create the impression that judges on the whole are doing too much to limit government when in fact they are doing far too little.

Judicial engagement is not activism; it is consistency in judging. If the government must have a valid reason for exercising power over individuals in some cases, then it should have a valid reason in all cases.

If it must exercise that power with care in some cases, then it should have to do so in all cases. If facts and evidence matter in some cases, then they should matter in all cases. Above all, courts should not be in the business of deciding that some constitutional rights deserve meaningful protection while others do not. But that is precisely what they are doing.

Critics charge that activist judges are rewriting the Constitution to create rights that do not exist or were never meant to be protected. But they often overlook the way that courts, over the years, have effectively amended the Constitution through judicial abdication: granting to government powers it does not legitimately possess and allowing public officials to wield excessive and often arbitrary authority over individuals. That is wrong, and we must put a stop to it. The Founders envisioned America as a land of liberty, a beacon of hope in a world blighted by tyranny and oppression. But liberty requires constitutionally limited government, which is impossible without judges who appreciate those limits and are fully committed to enforcing them.

This book presents the case for judicial engagement. The first two chapters begin by explaining how the Constitution was designed to limit government power and how the Supreme Court has undermined the Framers' plan by picking and choosing which constitutional limits it will enforce. Chapters 3 through 5 describe several specific examples of judicial abdication, including the use of rational basis review to rubber-stamp interference with "nonfundamental" rights, and the Supreme Court's almost infinitely elastic conception of federal power. Chapters 6 and 7 offer some thoughts about why judges appear so reluctant to fully enforce constitutional limits on government power, including the specter of judicial activism. Chapter 8 explains what judicial engagement would look like in practice and why there is little to fear from a judiciary that provides real judging in all constitutional cases. Finally, Chapter 9 concludes with some specific ideas for developing a more engaged judiciary.

CHAPTER 1

Constitutional Law for
Ordinary People

Why do we have a constitution at all? Why not Athenian-style direct democracy or a representative government with the power to do whatever politicians think best? Very simply, it's because government is not your friend. It is not your mother, your father, or a benevolent uncle. Nor is it your partner, your colleague, or your teammate. As far as the government is concerned, it is your boss, setting policies and issuing edicts that you *will* obey. Between that awesome power and you stands the Constitution. This chapter explains how the Constitution was designed to limit government by locking it up inside a fence and providing individuals with a suit of armor for when it sneaks out.

But first, let's take a closer look at the *why*—why is government not always on your side? The simple answer is that the government has strong incentives to advance its own interests, even at the expense of yours. Just ask the Caswell family, which owns a budget motel just inside the I-495 loop in Tewksbury, Massachusetts.

The Motel Caswell provides no-frills accommodations for people who can't afford the Motel 6 down the street. Over the years, a tiny percentage of guests have been arrested for committing crimes while staying at the motel, including minor drug crimes. Police reports show a similar number of drug-related arrests at other local businesses, including the Motel 6 and the parking lot of a nearby

Wal-Mart.[1] But the U.S. Department of Justice and the Tewksbury Police Department singled out the Motel Caswell and tried to take it using civil asset forfeiture.

Civil asset forfeiture is a process that enables law enforcement agencies to seize property connected with certain illegal activities but without arresting, let alone convicting, anyone of an actual crime. The legal standards are quite lax, and agencies frequently get to keep a portion of the proceeds from seized property, which can warp both their priorities and their incentives. Indeed, that may be why DOJ and the Tewksbury police zeroed in on the Motel Caswell: it's worth about $1.5 million, has no mortgage, and, being owned by a working-class family instead of a national chain, would be less able to defend itself from heavy-handed forfeiture tactics. *Ka-ching!*

Fortunately, the Institute for Justice stepped in to represent the Caswells for free just as they were running out of money to pay their mounting legal bills. At trial in November 2012, the government's case boiled down to an assertion that the Caswells should have done more to discourage people from committing drug crimes in the privacy of their own rooms. But there was no evidence that the Caswells even knew about most of those crimes, and in fact the Caswells did everything the police asked of them and more, including copying guests' driver's licenses at check-in, providing rooms to Tewksbury police officers to conduct surveillance, installing security cameras and additional lighting on the property, and staffing the front desk around the clock. If anything else should have been done to discourage drug crime at the motel, no one from the government ever said so.

In a thorough and carefully reasoned opinion, Judge Judith Dein, a U.S. magistrate judge, took the government to task for its ham-fisted attempt to seize the Motel Caswell. Not only did the government fail to establish a "substantial connection" between the motel and illicit drug use, as the law required, but the Caswells' complete cooperation with law enforcement in trying to prevent those activities entitled them to an "innocent owner" defense as well. With studied understatement, Judge

Dein said she found it "rather remarkable" that instead of working with the Caswells to implement further security measures or exclude particular guests, the government's first and only step was to try to take their motel. "Having failed to notify Mr. Caswell that he had a significant problem," she admonished, "and having failed to take any steps to advise him on what to do, the Government's resolution of the crime problem should not be to simply take his Property."[2]

As documented in the Institute for Justice report *Policing for Profit*, the government's mistreatment of the Caswells is not exceptional.[3] Perverse financial incentives and over-criminalization—i.e., using criminal law to punish harmless and often morally blameless conduct—have combined to erode the line between law enforcement and legalized theft.

Consider what happened to Kyle Jones and his family, who experienced civil forfeiture firsthand at Houston's George Bush Intercontinental Airport in June 2011, on their way to visit relatives in Ethiopia. Federal law required them to state whether they were carrying more than $10,000 in "monetary instruments," and if so, how much. When asked by a Homeland Security agent how much he had on him, Kyle said he didn't know exactly but "he would guess around $20,200." The agent wrote that amount on a form and told Kyle to sign it, which he did. The agent then pulled the family out of line and had them place their money on a table. Kyle had $20,000 in traveler's checks and $11,131 in cash, while his wife Berekti had $4,000 in cash—perfectly reasonable amounts for a two-month trip to see family in a country with a primarily cash economy. But Homeland Security agents seized the money anyway on the grounds that Kyle had violated federal law by failing to report the full amount. Incredibly, the government tried to defend the seizure in court, apparently seeing nothing wrong with the dishonest and manipulative behavior of the Homeland Security agents. In a scathing order that described the agents as "rascals" who "bullied" the Jones family, a federal judge ordered the government to return the money and pay the family's attorney's fees.[4]

Although the Caswell and Jones cases ended well, both families were traumatized by the conduct of government officials who were more focused on taking their property than respecting their constitutional rights. Both families also received top-flight legal representation and the kind of judicial engagement this book advocates for all cases. As we shall see, most victims of overweening government are not so fortunate.

The Constitution was designed to protect citizens from precisely the sort of government bullying that the Caswell and Jones families endured. To understand how, let's take a quick look at two of its most basic features.

TO "SECURE THE BLESSINGS OF LIBERTY"

The Constitution is a rulebook that tells us what the government may and may not do. Besides creating a federal government and explaining how it will operate, the Constitution imposes significant limits on government power at all levels—federal, state, and local. Among the most challenging and important issues in constitutional law is determining precisely what those limits are and how they should be enforced. For example, can the government kick you out of your home, bulldoze it, and give your property to someone else to build a more expensive home? Can a city charge one homeowner thirty times more than his neighbor for a sewer hookup just because it would be inconvenient to apportion the costs more fairly? Can regulators make it a crime to sell milk below a certain price set by the government?

The Supreme Court has said the Constitution allows government to do all of those things.[5] I think that's wrong, and I think most Americans would agree. Indeed, people across the country and on both sides of the political spectrum were outraged in 2005 when the Supreme Court upheld the use of eminent domain by the City of New London, Connecticut, to demolish the working-class neighborhood of Fort Trumbull and turn the land over to a property developer to build more expensive homes and an upscale hotel. As Justice Thomas said in his dissent in that case, *Kelo v. City of New London*, "Something has gone seriously awry with this Court's interpretation of the Constitution."[6]

It certainly has. Properly understood, the Constitution provides for much less government and far more freedom than the Supreme Court says it does. But to understand how the courts are getting it wrong, we must first understand how the Framers got it right. Two principles lie at the heart of their constitutional vision.

The first is that government may act only where it has the authority to do so. As noted earlier, one can imagine this principle as a fence that surrounds government and permits it to act only within the fenced area. You might think of it this way: If you were given a ticket for listening to your car radio while driving, you wouldn't challenge that ticket on the grounds that you have a constitutional right to listen to your car radio (even though you may). Instead, you'd challenge the ticket on the grounds that there is no law against listening to the radio while driving and therefore nobody—neither the local sheriff, the state police, nor the National Transportation Safety Board—has the authority to cite you for it.

The second principle at the heart of the Framers' vision is respect for individual rights, which I have described as a suit of armor that surrounds and protects each person from illegitimate government interference. Exactly which rights the Constitution protects and to what extent it protects them are difficult questions about which reasonable people may disagree. But the basic premise that people have rights that can trump government power is not seriously disputed, at least in America.

The remainder of the chapter explains the Constitution's commitment to these two principles and finishes with a short discussion of three overarching assumptions that strike me as essentially uncontroversial, but worth noting. Those assumptions are: (1) the Constitution is a legitimate source of political authority; (2) the institution of judicial review, by which courts claim the power to declare unconstitutional the actions of other branches, is also legitimate; and (3) judges should base their decisions on the text of the Constitution rather than their own beliefs about sound public policy.

GOVERNMENT FENCED IN

When Americans want to challenge the legitimacy of government action, they usually talk about rights. We are used to hearing people say things like: "I have the right to free speech!" "The Second Amendment protects my right to own a gun!" "I have the right to an attorney!" And while the Constitution certainly does protect those rights, I would urge fans of limited government to start elsewhere. Start with whether the government even has the authority to act in the first place. Chief Justice Roberts emphasized this point in his opinion upholding the federal health-care law in 2012: "Today, the restrictions on government power foremost in many Americans' minds are likely to be affirmative prohibitions such as contained in the Bill of Rights. These affirmative prohibitions come into play, however, *only where the Government possesses authority to act in the first place.*"[7] Although I disagree with his conclusion that the Constitution gives Congress the power to micromanage Americans' health-care decisions the way it did in the Affordable Care Act, Roberts was certainly correct that the most fundamental question in any constitutional case is not whether the citizen has a *right* to do X, but whether the government even has the *authority* to regulate X in the first place.

Imagine you told your kids you'd take them to a baseball game this Sunday, but you decide to spend the day on a municipal golf course instead. The city that operates the course can certainly keep you off the links for some reasons—being drunk or driving your golf cart onto the putting green, for example—but not because you promised your kids you'd spend the day with them. Enforcing noncontractual family agreements is simply not a legitimate end of government, and there is no law (how could there be?) against disappointing your children.

Given our tendency to focus on rights, it might seem strange to argue that in any constitutional case we should first consider the government's authority. But it's not strange at all. In fact, that's why the Constitution had no bill of rights when it went into effect in 1789. Did the absence of a bill of rights between 1789 and 1791 mean there were no limits on what laws the federal government could enact beyond the small handful of rights specifically mentioned in the original Constitution? Not at all. The Framers believed that the most effective way to protect liberty was not to create a list of specific rights that the government could not infringe, but instead to create a finite list of powers that the government could exercise. We call these "enumerated powers," and the ones delegated to the federal government are specifically set forth in the Constitution, mostly in Article I, Section 8. The Framers' intent to maximize the amount of space for liberty while minimizing the space for government is unmistakable. Put yourself in a shark cage and you have only a few inches of room to swim around. Put the shark in the cage and the rest of the ocean is yours.

Remember the case with the U.S. Department of Agriculture pestering the Hemingway museum about its cats? Instead of trying to anticipate the need for a constitutional right to care for one's own pets, the Framers' idea was to limit government by giving it certain specified powers only, while leaving everything else to the states or to individuals.[8] The powers of the federal government are listed in some detail, and they include things like coining money and punishing pirates. Supervising pet care is not among them. That ingenious plan for limiting government—focusing first on its legitimate powers—requires a properly engaged judiciary to implement. Unfortunately for the museum and its cats, we don't always get one.

So the powers of the federal government are, at least in principle, limited to those listed in the text of the Constitution. But what about state governments? With them, it's different. Unlike the federal government, the powers of state governments are not specifically enumerated, either in the U.S. Constitution or in their own state constitutions. This leads some to believe that the authority of state governments is plenary, subject only to the handful of restrictions in the text of the original Constitution and the Bill of Rights, along with any additional rights contained in state constitutions.

That is incorrect. There is another major limit on the power of state governments, and while the explanation is a bit complicated, I think most Americans have a strong intuitive grasp that it must be so. Earlier, I explained that a police officer cannot give you a ticket for listening to your car radio because there is no law against doing so, and the government cannot kick you off a municipal golf course for failing to take your kids to a baseball game because preventing parents from disappointing their children is not a legitimate function of government. It turns out there are all kinds of things that state and local officials have no authority to do. Sometimes they lack the authority because there is no law on the books giving it to them; other times they lack the authority because the particular thing they are trying to do is not among the legitimate powers of any state government.

The Institute for Justice made the former point in a case involving a massage therapist named Mercedes Clemens. Mercedes loves horses and her massage practice in Maryland includes both people and horses. Everything was going fine until Mercedes received a letter from the Maryland Board of Chiropractic and Massage Therapy Examiners ordering her to "discontinue her animal massage practice" because the board had licensed her only to provide *human* massage therapy. Mercedes pointed out that Maryland had no laws regarding animal massage and therefore it was none of the board's business whether she treated horses as well as humans. But the board was unmoved. So Mercedes went to court, and a state trial judge agreed with her, holding that the board "*lacked authority* to issue the cease and desist order in this case."[9]

In Mercedes' case, the massage board's lack of authority flowed from the absence of any state statute empowering it to regulate the practice of animal massage. But there are constitutional limits on the

powers of state governments as well, including a baseline requirement that states may only pursue permissible government ends. What
are the constitutionally permissible ends of state governments? It's
a challenging question because, as noted above, the powers of state
governments are not specifically enumerated the way the federal
government's powers are. Instead, state governments have something
called the "police power," which, though broad, is nevertheless limited in scope.

The police power involves more than the ability to put people in
jail for committing crimes, as its name might imply. It refers to all of
the ends (or "objects," as the Supreme Court sometimes calls them)
that state governments may properly pursue. Some ends are plainly
legitimate, like protecting public health and safety. And some ends are
plainly illegitimate, like singling people out for adverse treatment on
the basis of personal animosity or their failure to pay a bribe.

That's precisely what happened in a case called *Cruz v. Town of
Cicero*, involving several entrepreneurs who were in the business of
buying multi-family apartment buildings, refurbishing them, and selling
individual units as condominiums.[10] This required various permits
from the town government, which were forthcoming at first but then
suddenly were not. At trial, it came out that the town president had
solicited a bribe from the entrepreneurs to ensure that they continued
receiving the necessary permits. When the bribe wasn't paid, the
permits stopped coming. From these facts, the court concluded that
the town president was attempting to "serve her personal ends" by
using her power over the permitting process to shake down local busi-
nessmen.[11] The court held that particular use of government power to
be unconstitutional even though nothing in the Constitution specifically prohibits graft or expressly mentions the right to own a business,
sell condominiums, or earn a living. The reason the town president's
actions were found unconstitutional is because shaking down citizens
for bribes is not a permissible use of government power—what courts
call a "legitimate state interest."

Deciding whether a given state interest is legitimate or illegitimate can be easy or hard, depending on the case. It is a question to which the Supreme Court has devoted surprisingly little attention. Justice Scalia has observed, "Our cases have not elaborated on the standards for determining what constitutes a 'legitimate state interest.'"[12] The reason may be, in part, that government officials sometimes pursue ends—such as graft, suppressing dissent, avoiding accountability, and punishing personal or political opponents—that are so obviously illegitimate there seems little point in trying to explain why. But other cases are much more difficult. Indeed, as Professor Randy Barnett notes in his indispensable book *Restoring the Lost Constitution*, determining the scope of the police power is "one of the most challenging and vexatious issues in constitutional theory."[13] Readers who are interested in knowing more about how the U.S. Constitution restricts the scope of the state police power should read Chapter 12 of Professor Barnett's book, where he presents a compelling argument that the state police power is limited in scope.[14] Suffice it to say his conclusion squares with the intuitions of ordinary Americans and judges alike that there are some things the government simply may not do, such as prevent us from running a business or building a home unless we pay a bribe. In any constitutional case, the requirement must always be on government to establish that it is pursuing a permissible end. Only then do we reach the question of whether the government's action violates some particular individual right.

To summarize, governments may only pursue constitutionally legitimate ends. For the federal government, these ends are specifically listed, or "enumerated," in the text of the Constitution. The constitutionally permissible ends of state governments, though broader, are limited as well. They do not include things like graft, economic protectionism, or sheer animus toward disfavored groups. Determining what other government ends lie outside the legitimate scope of the police power can certainly be a challenge, but that does not excuse courts from making the effort, as they typically do not in cases involving certain disfavored rights like earning a living or running a business.

GOVERNMENT FENCED OUT

Besides confining its actions to permissible ends, the government must also respect people's individual rights. In other words, even when government is operating inside the "fence" represented by its constitutionally authorized powers, it must exercise those powers in a way that does not invade the "armor" of individual rights that surrounds every person.

Figuring out just which rights the Constitution protects is, like the scope of the police power, a difficult question. And even when we determine that a given right should be protected, the question remains: to what extent? To say that the government may not "abridge" the freedom of speech or "infringe" the right to bear arms does not mean those rights cannot be regulated at all. But drawing the line between permissible regulation and impermissible infringement can be quite challenging—so much so that courts have largely abandoned the effort in many areas of constitutional law in favor of a simplistic judge-by-labels approach, as we shall see.

At the outset, then, there are two questions to answer: *which* rights does the Constitution protect, and to what *extent* does it protect those rights from government regulation? I address the first question below and the second in the following chapter.

WRITTEN AND UNWRITTEN RIGHTS

The Constitution specifically identifies various individual rights, both in the main body and in various amendments. Among other things, the Constitution provides that: habeas corpus may not be suspended except in cases of rebellion or invasion; states may not impair the obligation of contracts; Congress may not prohibit the free exercise of religion; the right to keep and bear arms shall not be infringed; cruel and unusual punishments may not be inflicted.[15] Those rights can be read broadly or narrowly, but either way, there is a clear textual basis for enforcing them.

But does the Constitution also protect rights that are not specifically set forth in its text—what courts call "unenumerated" rights? The Supreme Court says yes, and we know from experience that the consequences of not protecting at least some unenumerated rights would be appalling. It is impossible to predict all the ways in which government might misbehave, and if we allow it to get away with doing what no one ever thought to prohibit specifically, the results can be—indeed, have often been—horrendous. As a result, even people who denounce unenumerated rights in theory nevertheless tend to embrace them in practice, presumably because they understand how monstrous it would be if they did not, and because they have no wish to marginalize themselves into irrelevance by embracing the consequences that flow from their stated opposition to unenumerated rights.

To appreciate why it's so difficult to say precisely which rights the Constitution protects, imagine you were assigned the task of creating a list of judicially enforceable rights from scratch. What would they be? Should you include such pedestrian things as eating, sleeping, or wearing clothes, or would that be ridiculous? What about raising your own children or taking medicine when you're sick—too obvious? How about wearing a hat or going fishing—too trivial?[16] It's a mindboggling challenge when you think about it, and the stakes are even higher when you realize that some people will argue that any rights you didn't list should not be protected.

In fact, that was precisely the concern the Framers had, and it is why James Madison initially resisted the idea of including a bill of rights in the Constitution. But popular demand for a bill of rights was clear, so Congress took up the task immediately following ratification. As Professor Barnett and others have documented, the debates over what rights to include are illuminating. For example, Representative Theodore Sedgwick believed the right of assembly was so "self-evident" that it would be "derogatory to the dignity of the House to descend to such minutiae" by including it in a bill of rights. If such an obvious right were to be included, he argued, why not also "declare[] that a man should have a right to wear his hat if he pleased; that he might get up when he pleased, and go to bed when he thought proper"?[17] This echoed a point made earlier by the future Supreme Court justice James Iredell to the North Carolina ratification convention in defending the Framers' initial decision not to include a bill of rights: "Let any one make what collection or enumeration of rights he pleases, I will immediately mention twenty or thirty more rights not contained in it."[18]

James Madison devised an elegant solution to that problem, and he did so with the specific purpose of preempting the argument that any rights not specifically listed in the Constitution should not be protected. Thus, the Ninth Amendment provides that "[t]he enumeration in the Constitution of certain rights shall not be construed to deny or disparage others retained by the people." Given the amendment's unambiguous text, purpose, and history, those who dispute the concept of judicially enforceable unenumerated rights carry a heavy burden of persuasion. The same is true of another constitutional amendment, the Fourteenth, which contains even more explicit protections for unenumerated rights.

The Supreme Court held in an 1833 case, *Barron v. Baltimore*,[19] that the Bill of Rights did not apply directly to state and local governments. As a result, there was nothing in the Constitution to prevent states from abridging the freedom of speech, and in fact it was quite common for Southern states in particular to censor speech advocating the abolition of slavery. Even though most state constitutions included specific protections for individual rights, including speech, state courts often failed to enforce those provisions. Infringements of individual liberty by state and local governments were so widespread following the Civil War that Congress passed several laws seeking to protect the basic civil rights of all citizens, white and black. When questions arose about the federal government's authority to enforce those laws, Congress proposed the Fourteenth Amendment to remove any doubt.

Section 1 of the Fourteenth Amendment contains three key protections of individual rights: it provides that no state may deprive any person of life, liberty, or property without due process of law; that no state may deny anyone equal protection of the laws; and that states may not abridge the privileges or immunities of United States citizens. Precisely what rights the privileges or immunities clause was meant to protect remains unclear because the Supreme Court effectively deleted that language from the Fourteenth Amendment in an 1873 decision called the *Slaughter-House Cases*. *Slaughter-House* represents a particularly glaring example of judicial abdication, as we shall see in Chapter 5. For now, it is enough to note that the Supreme Court tried to compensate for its misreading of the Fourteenth Amendment in *Slaughter-House* by shifting much of the work that the privileges or immunities clause was designed to do—namely, protecting an array of individual rights from violation by state and local governments—onto the due process and equal protection clauses. Often this involves the use of a legal doctrine called "substantive due process," which strikes some people as an oxymoron: how can a provision that protects due *process* of law be interpreted to impose *substantive* limits on government power?

In fact, the historical and textual arguments for substantive due process are quite strong, even if some legal authorities disparage the concept.[20] But putting aside that somewhat academic debate, the more telling point is that even the staunchest opponents of unenumerated rights end up embracing them when push comes to shove. And whether they do so as a matter of substantive due process, as the Supreme Court does, or the privileges or immunities clause, which was actually designed for that purpose, the result is that virtually everyone seems to agree that courts should protect at least some unenumerated rights.

So why do people who deride the concept of unenumerated rights in theory typically end up embracing it, however grudgingly, in practice? As noted before, I suspect it has much to do with the monstrous implications of protecting only those rights specifically set forth in the Constitution. There are many possible illustrations, but a handful will suffice.

Eugenics was widely practiced throughout the United States in the first half of the twentieth century. More than half the states had laws on the books at one time or another authorizing the government to sterilize various groups of people, including habitual criminals and the "socially inadequate." More than sixty thousand people were sterilized over a period of roughly seventy years, many of them young minority women. The Supreme Court upheld this practice in a 1927 case called *Buck v. Bell*.[21] The opinion was written by a champion of judicial restraint, Oliver Wendell Holmes Jr. At issue was whether the State of Virginia could sterilize eighteen-year-old Carrie Buck, whom Justice Holmes described as a "feeble-minded white woman" who was the "daughter of a feeble-minded mother . . . and the mother of an illegitimate feeble-minded child."[22] Citing a recent Supreme Court decision upholding a mandatory vaccination law from Massachusetts, Holmes argued: "The principle that sustains compulsory vaccination is broad enough to cover cutting the Fallopian tubes. Three generations of imbeciles are enough."[23]

Similarly, it was once a crime in many states to marry outside one's race. There is nothing in the text of the Constitution that explicitly protects the right to marry at all, let alone outside one's own race. And because such anti-miscegenation laws apply equally to members of all races, they do not technically discriminate against anyone. As a result, the Supreme Court upheld the practice in *Pace v. Alabama*,[24] a doleful example of judicial restraint that stood for more than eighty years until it was finally overturned in *Loving v. Virginia* (1967).[25]

Another item missing from the bullet-point Constitution is the right to have and raise one's own children. This is a question—unlike eugenic sterilization and interracial marriage—that the Supreme Court got right from the very beginning, striking down an Oregon law that prohibited parents from sending their children to private school and a Nebraska law that made it illegal to teach children in any other language but English.[26] In the latter case, *Meyer v. Nebraska* (1923), Justice James McReynolds held that the "liberty" protected by the Fourteenth Amendment's due process clause "denotes not merely freedom from bodily restraint but also the right of the individual to contract, to engage in any of the common occupations of life, to acquire useful knowledge, to marry, establish a home and bring up children . . . and generally to enjoy those privileges long recognized at common law as essential to the orderly pursuit of happiness by free men."[27]

In providing these examples I am not arguing that the Constitution should be interpreted to protect unenumerated rights just because the consequences of doing otherwise would be unacceptable. Instead, my argument is: (a) the textual and historical reasons for concluding that the Constitution was meant to protect unenumerated rights are quite strong; (b) those arguments have generally been given short shrift by minimalists who prefer a narrower role for the courts; and (c) it is reasonable to discount the arguments of critics who have no persuasive explanation for why they selectively embrace the concept of unenumerated rights in practice while disparaging it in theory. In any event, my perception is that most people agree in practice that the real question is not *whether* the Constitution protects unenumerated rights, but *which* unenumerated rights it protects. Instead of tackling that question head-on, however, the Supreme Court has tried to fudge it with a jurisprudential gimmick called the rational basis test, as will be discussed in the next two chapters.

THREE ASSUMPTIONS

I conclude with three assumptions that underlie the call for judicial engagement but strike me as sufficiently well accepted that there is little point in dwelling on them.

First, I assume that the Constitution is a legitimate source of political authority. By this I mean the Constitution establishes a legal framework that determines what actions the government may properly take and what actions it may not. Government officials are bound to obey the Constitution, and they must conform their actions to the limits it provides. By the same token, citizens should consider as lawful (though not necessarily just or wise) government policies that comport with the Constitution.

Second, I assume it is appropriate for judges to determine the unconstitutionality of government action, which is the purest form of judicial review. Thus, if a government agency claims the authority to do something—installing GPS tracking devices on people's cars without a warrant and recording their every move for months at a time, let's say—and the Supreme Court finds it unconstitutional (which it did),[28] then the government must obey that ruling. This is not to say that members of other branches have no independent obligation to exercise their own constitutional judgment; they do. If a legislator thinks a given bill is unconstitutional then she should not vote for it, nor should the president sign a bill he believes to be unconstitutional, regardless of what the courts might say.[29]

The latter point is worth elaborating since it appears to be the source of some confusion. It is not accurate to equate judicial review with "judicial supremacy." That's because all three branches have a role to play in constitutional interpretation.[30] Thus, if the Supreme Court mistakenly holds that a given policy is constitutional—as I believe it does with some regularity—members of the other branches can and should make their own independent determination about whether the policy is constitutionally permissible. But when a court determines that a given law or policy is *unconstitutional*, the other branches should accept that ruling, as they nearly always have throughout our nation's history. To do otherwise would be to allow members of the legislative and executive branches to have the final say regarding the propriety of their own conduct, which violates the basic maxim of just govern-ment that no man may be a judge in his own case.[31]

Finally, I assume that judges should base their rulings on the text of the Constitution instead of their own policy preferences—an approach that is often referred to as "textualism" to distinguish it from an approach in which the judge is guided more by her own percep-tions of justice or sound policy. This is not to say that judges should disregard the potential consequences of their rulings or that they may not look to other sources for clarification, particularly when applying broadly worded constitutional provisions like "due process" or "equal protection" to particular cases. These and other provisions, like the Fourth Amendment's prohibition against "unreasonable" searches, involve value-laden terms about which reasonable people can disagree. Reasonable people can also disagree about what sources judges may legitimately consult when applying such terms to particular cases. This doesn't mean that all constitutional questions are inherently subjective or value-laden (the requirement that the president be at least thirty-five years old seems clear enough), but it underscores the fact that the Constitution is not a tape measure. Still, it's not a bungee cord either, and judges should honor its text.

By assuming these premises, I do not mean to suggest they are incontestable. Indeed, each of them has been challenged in provoca-tive ways. Professor Barnett addresses some of these challenges in *Restoring the Lost Constitution*, a substantial portion of which he devotes to the question of legitimacy and why the Constitution is binding in conscience even though no living American actually consented to it.[32] Judicial review has come in for even more criticism, as has the idea that we should allow ourselves to be ruled by the "dead hand" of people who wrote the Constitution more than two centuries ago.

The reason I assume the legitimacy of the Constitution, judicial review, and textualism is that I believe the most important battles in constitutional law are being fought elsewhere. When people disagree about the constitutionality of things like abortion or gay marriage, they rarely start by questioning the legitimacy of the Constitution itself, or whether courts have an appropriate role in interpreting it, or whether judges should embrace or ignore the text of the Constitution in answering those questions. I say "rarely" because it does happen occasionally, but usually in an inconsistent and opportunistic way. Here is one example.

Mark Levin is a best-selling author and nationally syndicated conservative radio host. I agree with him on many points, especially about limiting government power. But I am puzzled by the treatment of judicial review in his book *Men in Black: How the Supreme Court Is Destroying America*. Levin devotes an entire chapter to the proposition that judicial review was specifically considered and rejected by the Framers but then resurrected by the courts through an act of judicial "tyranny."[33] He argues that "[n]either the history of our founding nor the establishment of our government supports the current arrangement in which the judiciary rules supreme."[34] And yet in the same book, Levin excoriates the Supreme Court for failing to strike down various laws, including New Deal programs that vastly expanded federal control of the economy, the executive order allowing the internment of Japanese Americans during World War II, campaign finance laws, and affirmative action.[35] And he doesn't just argue that those decisions were wrong. He describes the Supreme Court's federalism jurisprudence as "socialism from the bench" and the failure to strike down affirmative action programs and campaign finance laws as "endorsing racism" and "silencing political debate," respectively.[36]

Well, which is it? Judicial review is either legitimate or it is not. But it cannot be legitimate in some cases (those where you disagree with a given policy and would like to see it blocked) and illegitimate in others (those where you support the policy and wish to see it enforced without judicial interference). Moreover, given the tone of his denunciations, it does not seem plausible to me that Levin is simply arguing that if the courts are going to exercise the illegitimate power of judicial review, then they should at least get it right. Instead, Levin seems to feel that when courts fail to enforce a particular constitutional limit on government power, they are in some sense complicit in the resulting infringement of liberty. If so, I strongly agree, and I think it is no accident that self-professed opponents of judicial review tend to embrace that view only sporadically.

Moreover, most Americans appear deeply committed to the institution of judicial review, even if they might not always like the results it produces. They expect the courts to serve as a check on government power, as the leading Framers repeatedly indicated was part of their plan for limited government. People tend to be disappointed and even outraged when the Supreme Court abdicates that responsibility, as it did when it allowed the government to relocate Japanese Americans in *Korematsu v. United States*,[37] and again in *Kelo v. City of New London*[38] when it upheld the use of eminent domain to take homes and businesses from law-abiding citizens and give them to a private property developer.

Most people have a strong conviction that the government violated the Constitution in those cases even though the Supreme Court said it did not. That conviction is correct, and it is based on a fundamental intuition about the nature of just government, which is this: Government should have a good reason for restricting people's freedom or taking what belongs to them. Whether it is putting people in jail, bulldozing their homes, or making them pass a test to sell flower arrangements, the government owes people an honest explanation and a measure of care in restricting their freedom. As we shall see in the next two chapters, courts enforce that basic obligation in some cases but not others.

CHAPTER 2

How Courts Protect Rights
They Care About

The Supreme Court divides your rights into two distinct categories that it calls "fundamental" and "nonfundamental." Fundamental rights receive meaningful judicial protection; nonfundamental rights do not.

Thus, government must have a good reason for interfering with a fundamental right like speech, voting, or religion. On the other hand, rights the Supreme Court considers nonfundamental—such as earning a living, or not having one's house taken through eminent domain—may be infringed for pretty much any reason, even ones the government dreams up after the fact in order to justify its conduct. But in fact there are no unimportant rights, nor is there any class of cases in which the government should be allowed to misrepresent its conduct while judges turn a blind eye to its true ends. Unfortunately, the Supreme Court has held otherwise, and the result is a sharp dichotomy between those constitutional rights that judges will actually protect and those to which they merely pay lip service.

MEANINGFUL AND MEANINGLESS RIGHTS

As noted in the last chapter, courts have struggled with two basic questions about rights: which ones does the Constitution protect, and to what extent? All constitutional rights are subject to at least some regulation. For instance, the First Amendment does not protect the right to run fraudulent advertisements or smear a person's reputation with lies. But it does protect the right to criticize politicians, notwithstanding their occasional desire to blunt or suppress such criticism. Similarly, while the Second Amendment specifically protects the right to keep and bear arms, that certainly does not include nuclear weapons. So where should courts draw the line between permissible regulation and impermissible infringement of rights, and how vigilant should they be in policing that line?

Those are tough questions, and the Supreme Court has tried to dodge them by creating a distinction between "fundamental" and "nonfundamental" rights. A meaningful (or fundamental) right is one you have a fair chance of vindicating in court before a judge who will think and act like a truly neutral adjudicator. Meaningless rights, which the courts refer to as nonfundamental (or, even more euphemistically, as mere "liberty interests"), are ones you do not have much chance of vindicating because the judge will act more like an advocate for the government than an impartial referee.

Characterizing rights as fundamental or nonfundamental is an essentially arbitrary process designed to replace actual judgment with more of a paint-by-numbers approach. Once he decides which box a given right goes into, a judge basically knows—which is to say, preordains—the outcome of the case.[1]

Most of the rights specifically mentioned in the Constitution have been deemed fundamental by the Supreme Court. They include free speech, the right to assemble and petition the government, free exercise of religion, and various protections for criminal defendants listed in the Fifth and Sixth Amendments, like the right to counsel. Besides these, there are a handful of unenumerated rights that the Supreme Court considers sufficiently "rooted in the Nation's history and tradition" to warrant meaningful judicial protection as well.[2] These include the right to marry, to have or not have children, to direct the upbringing of one's children, and the right to travel within the United States.[3]

Designating a right as "fundamental" is the exception, not the rule. As a result, the vast majority of things you might want to do on any given day—from making breakfast in the morning to going shopping after work or taking your kids for a swim at the pool—involve nonfundamental rights that the government may regulate virtually at will. And it's not just little things like whether you may grow vegetables in your yard or drink raw milk if you prefer.[4] Courts have also declared "nonfundamental" such rights as the ability to seek life-saving medical care, work in the occupation of one's choice, and choose whom to live with.[5]

HOW COURTS PROTECT RIGHTS THEY CARE ABOUT

Rights deemed fundamental receive real judging—what this book calls judicial engagement. The hallmark of engaged judging is a genuine search for truth by a neutral adjudicator on the basis of reliable evidence. A properly engaged judge refuses to accept the government's self-serving justifications at face value, but instead seeks to determine the government's true ends, to ensure they are constitutionally permissible. The engaged judge also considers the relationship between the government's stated objective and the means chosen to pursue it. There must be a reasonable fit between ends and means; among other things, a poor fit may indicate that the government is pursuing an objective other than the one it claims.

Courts are quite familiar with engaged judging and perfectly comfortable applying it in a wide variety of cases. Indeed, weighing evidence, evaluating the credibility of witnesses, and distinguishing truth from baseless, self-serving rationalizations is precisely what judges do in nonjury civil cases involving things like breach of contract or medical malpractice, where one party has the burden of proving, typically by a preponderance of the evidence, the elements of whatever claims or defenses they are trying to establish. Courts seem comfortable with that sort of judicial engagement in many constitutional settings as well, including cases featuring "fundamental" rights such as free speech and the free exercise of religion, as well as the right not to be discriminated against on the basis of race or gender. In those cases, judges routinely assess the veracity of the government's explanations for its conduct and refuse to accept justifications for which the government has no evidence or that are demonstrably pretextual—such as when the City of Hialeah, Florida, claimed that it had banned ritual sacrifice on grounds of animal cruelty, when in fact the true "object" of the law, as determined by the Supreme Court, was the "suppression of the central element of the Santeria worship service."[6]

Regrettably, Hialeah's lack of candor about its actual reason for enacting the law was not an isolated case. Experience and observation make perfectly clear that the government is not always honest about its true ends when defending the constitutionality of laws it has passed. In the Second Amendment area, for example, legislators may claim their purpose is to mitigate gun violence, but some laws and regulations seem more concerned with discouraging gun ownership. Thus, as the lawyers David Rivkin and Andrew Grossman explained in the *Wall Street Journal,* it appears that the "real purpose" behind proposals to make gun owners carry insurance is to "make guns less affordable for law-abiding citizens and thereby reduce private gun ownership."[7] In a recent case involving the constitutionality of taking warrantless "cheek swabs" of people who have been arrested, the Supreme Court accepted Maryland's assertion that its purpose was simply to identify those people, not to use their DNA to see whether they had committed other crimes. But as Justice Scalia remarked in his withering dissent, "The Court's assertion that DNA is being taken, not to solve crimes, but to *identify* those in the State's custody, taxes the credulity of the credulous."[8]

Yet another example of the government concealing its true ends arose in a campaign finance case that my colleague Bill Maurer argued before the Supreme Court in 2011. Arizona's Clean Elections Act provided government funding to political candidates who agreed not to accept private donations or use their own money to finance their campaigns. It also penalized nonparticipating candidates by awarding their opponents a disproportionate amount of money with which to respond whenever people ran ads against them. Through these and other gimmicks, the act was expressly designed to "level the playing field" among political candidates in Arizona. But because that is a constitutionally impermissible objective, the state had to disavow it. Asked by Chief Justice Roberts whether he agreed that "leveling the playing field for candidates is not a legitimate State purpose," one of the lawyers defending the law agreed, but said, "that, of course, is not what's at work here." To which Roberts memorably responded, "Well, I checked the Citizens Clean Elections Commission website this morning, and it says that this act was passed to, quote, 'level the playing field' when it comes to running for office."[9]

Some people argue that it isn't possible to determine the government's true ends or that evaluating the "fit" between the government's ends, whatever they may be, and the means chosen to advance them is hopelessly subjective. But there is no other way to do constitutional law. After all, if it were true that courts can neither discern the government's true "object" nor evaluate the "fit" between a given law and the government's legitimate objectives, then constitutional cases would necessarily turn on the government's willingness to misrepresent its true ends in court:

"So why did you pass this law banning the sacrifice of animals in religious ceremonies?"

"To stop the spread of bird flu and ensure a steady supply of Chicken McNuggets to the people of Florida. Oh, and also to prevent terrorists from using chicken carcasses as IEDs, but that information is classified."

"I see. Well then, carry on. Sorry to bother you."

I frequently encounter people who claim it is impossible to know what ends the government is actually pursuing with any given policy. But think what constitutional adjudication would look like if that argument were true: "Why did you firewall the whole Internet?" "National security." Done. "Why did you bulldoze Susette Kelo's home?" "National security." Done. "Why do you require a license to sell flowers?" "National security." Done. Is it really impossible to rule out national security (or, say, preventing avalanches or promoting dental hygiene) as possible objects of Louisiana's florist licensing law? Certainly not. The idea that it is any less possible to rule out consumer protection is a judicial invention—one that has far more to do with expedience than reality.

Moreover, courts practice engaged judging all the time in cases they care about. Take so-called "commercial speech" cases, for example, as noted in connection with the coconut-water hypothetical in the Introduction.

According to the Supreme Court, speech that proposes a transaction—what the Court calls "commercial speech"—is not entitled to the same level of protection as other forms of expression. Although the text of the Constitution provides no warrant for that distinction, commercial speech sits at the intersection of two conflicting strands of Supreme Court precedent: free expression, which the Court generally cares about very much, and economic liberty, which the Court generally cares about very little. As a result, government regulation of advertisements, promotional materials, and other forms of business-related speech receives a lower level of judicial review than regulation of speech in most other settings, but still a meaningful level.

In deciding whether the government may regulate truthful speech about a lawful product or service, a judge asks three questions: (1) Does the government have a "substantial interest" in restricting the speech? (2) Does the regulation actually advance that interest? (3) Is the law reasonably tailored so it doesn't restrict more speech than necessary?[10]

Significantly, the government bears the burden of proof on each of these points, and it must support its factual assertions with evidence rather than "speculation and conjecture."[11] That may seem like a rather modest requirement, and in fact it is. Consider whether making the government support its freedom-restricting policies with honest explanations and admissible evidence unfairly restricted its authority in the following two commercial speech cases, one involving a "For Sale" sign in Ohio and the other dealing with interior designers in Texas.

Christopher Pagan is a lawyer from Glendale, Ohio. In 2003, he accepted a 1970 Mercury Cougar XR7 as payment from a client in lieu of money. Not having any use for the car, he decided to sell it. Chris took out ads in the newspaper and online, but they didn't attract a buyer. So he put a "For Sale" sign in the car's window and parked it on the street in front of his house. And that made him a criminal.

That's because Glendale had a city ordinance that made it illegal to park your car on the street with a "For Sale" sign in it. Glendale police told Chris about the ordinance, which he'd never heard of, and ordered him to remove the sign. After doing a little research, Chris concluded that the law violated his First Amendment right to free speech, especially since it singled out "For Sale" signs while permitting signs with any other message, from "Save the Whales" to "Go Buckeyes!" Chris explained this to various city officials, but they would not relent. So he took down the sign and did what you might expect a lawyer to do. He went to court.

At first, things did not go well. The trial court ruled against him, and when Chris appealed the case, a three-judge panel initially ruled against him as well. But my colleague Jeff Rowes, who had just started at the Institute for Justice and had never even appeared in court, noted the ruling and decided it must be wrong. He then set about convincing all fifteen judges of the Sixth Circuit Court of Appeals to reconsider the case, which almost never happens. Besides being an exceptionally gifted lawyer, Jeff is a remarkably persuasive person, and he convinced the court to take a second look.

The city defended the law as a safety measure, arguing that it was designed to keep people from walking into traffic while "'looking over a motor vehicle which is displaying a for sale sign parked on the street.'"[12] The city had no evidence that this was a genuine concern, and relied instead on a bare assertion to that effect by its police chief. But that's not enough where meaningful rights like free speech are at stake. "If 'For Sale' signs are a threat to the physical safety of Glendale's citizens . . . ," the court majority noted in its opinion, "it seems no great burden to require Glendale to come forward with some evidence of the threat or the particular concerns."[13] No great burden, perhaps, but still more than the city could manage. Like a poker player caught bluffing, the city had to fold. And the number of pedestrians run over in the streets while looking at used cars in Glendale? Six years later, it still stands at zero.

Another example of engaged judging in a commercial speech case involved a Texas state law that allowed anyone to perform interior design work but required a special permit to use the term "interior design" or "interior designer." Since government is not normally allowed to censor truthful commercial speech, the state needed some explanation for why it was prohibiting people who lawfully performed interior design work from referring to themselves, accurately, as interior designers. The state's lawyers argued that allowing only those people who possessed specific credentials to refer to themselves as interior designers might help prevent customers from being misled about a given practitioner's true merits. There were several practical problems with that argument, including the fact that more than 80 percent of state-registered interior designers had been grandfathered in when the law was enacted and did not actually possess the requisite qualifications.

But the court focused on an even more fundamental point, which was the utter lack of fit between the legislature's stated goal of preventing consumer confusion and the means chosen to advance it. If the state were really concerned about providing potential customers with useful information, it could have chosen to regulate a more specific term, such as "*licensed* interior designer."[14] In reality, of course, the Texas interior design law had nothing to do with protecting consumers from being misled and everything to do with protecting state-registered interior designers from competition.[15]

Thus, despite the fact that commercial speech has been singled out for less protection than other forms of speech, it still receives a level of protection that reflects the basic hallmarks of judicial engagement: (1) figuring out what end the government is actually pursuing and making sure that end is constitutionally legitimate; (2) ensuring a reasonable fit between the government's actual end and the means chosen to advance it; and (3) requiring the government to justify its actions with something more than "speculation and conjecture."

WHEN COURTS CARED ABOUT OCCUPATIONAL FREEDOM

As noted above, commercial speech sits at the intersection of two distinct strands of constitutional law: free speech, which courts care about very much, and economic liberty, which courts used to care about but mostly don't anymore. Consider the most basic economic liberty, occupational freedom. The Supreme Court first recognized the right to earn an honest living more than a century ago, and it has acknowledged the existence of that right—even while withdrawing any meaningful protection for it—ever since.[16] Occupational freedom is an issue that comes up frequently because saddling entrepreneurs and businesses with anticompetitive regulations is a favorite way for government to curry favor with interest groups and dispense favors to political cronies, just as Texas did with its interior design law.[17]

Occupational licensing was virtually unknown in America for the first hundred years or so. But the late nineteenth century saw the sudden influx of three new groups into the labor market: newly freed blacks, women, and immigrants. Threatened by these new workers and resentful about having to compete with them for jobs, established interests—that is, native-born white males—used their political power to enact a raft of regulations designed to hamstring the newcomers. These regulations were clothed as public welfare measures, but the disguise often proved threadbare on closer inspection.

For example, San Francisco passed an ordinance in 1880 regulating laundries. The ordinance required everyone who operated a laundry to get a permit unless the facility was made of brick or stone. Since 97 percent of the laundries operating in San Francisco at the time were made of wood, just about everyone had to get a permit. Two Chinese men challenged the constitutionality of the ordinance after they were arrested for operating their laundries without a permit, which each had applied for unsuccessfully.

The California Supreme Court upheld the ordinance as a public safety measure designed to reduce the risk of fire. "Clothes-washing is certainly not opposed to good morals," the court acknowledged, but argued that "it may be highly dangerous to public safety," especially when carried on in a wooden building.[18] When the case, *Yick Wo v. Hopkins*, reached the U.S. Supreme Court, however, the justices took a closer look to see how the city's public safety rationale squared with the facts of the case. It turns out, not very well.

Among the facts not noted by the California Supreme Court in upholding the ordinance was that every Chinese person who applied for a permit to operate a wooden laundry was denied, while every white person, with a single exception, was approved. The justices therefore felt "constrained . . . to differ from the supreme court of California *upon the real meaning of the ordinances in question.*"[19] And whereas the California Supreme Court simply accepted at face value the city's representation that the ordinance was designed to prevent fires, the U.S. Supreme Court drew its own conclusion from "the facts shown" and determined that the only plausible explanation for the ordinance was "hostility" toward Chinese people, which is not a legitimate government interest.[20] Accordingly, the city's enforcement of the ordinance was held unconstitutional and the charges against the two men were dismissed.

At the same time San Francisco was trying to run Chinese people out of the laundry business and lying about it in court, back east the State of New York was trying to legislate immigrant cigar makers out of business, and misrepresenting its true ends as well.

Peter Jacobs was arrested on May 14, 1884, for violating a New York law that prohibited making cigars in a "tenement-house," defined as any building occupied by more than three families—what we would call an apartment building.[21] In a case called *In re Jacobs*, he challenged the constitutionality of the regulation, which the state sought to defend as a "health law."[22] Noting the strangely limited scope of the statute (it applied only in cities with a population of more than five hundred thousand, meaning Manhattan and Brooklyn)[23] and the lack of evidence that rolling cigars posed any genuine safety concerns, the New York Court of Appeals concluded, "It is plain that this is not a health law, and that it has no relation whatever to the public health."[24] The court rejected the idea that a legislative statement of purpose lent any support to the public health argument, reasoning that it is for the courts to determine whether the law "really relates to and is convenient and appropriate to protect the public health." And while the court did not speculate about the cigar-making law's actual purpose, Professor David Bernstein argues that "in fact, [it] was passed at the behest of the German-dominated Cigar Makers union to stifle competition from new Bohemian immigrants."[25]

Though it glossed over the law's true end, the court of appeals did emphasize the limitless nature of the state's conception of its own power. If all that is necessary to uphold the constitutionality of a law is for the government to *assert* that it serves a legitimate public purpose—and if that bare assertion is binding on the courts, no matter how implausible it might be as a matter of fact—then there is no limit to the government's authority. And thus,

> while far removed in time we will not be far away in practical statesmanship from those ages when governmental prefects

supervised the building of houses, the rearing of cattle, the sowing of seed and the reaping of grain, and governmental ordinances regulated the movements and labor of artisans, the rate of wages, the price of food, the diet and clothing of the people, and a large range of other affairs long since in all civilized lands regarded as outside of governmental functions.[26]

In other words, the only thing standing between us and legislative tyranny is a properly engaged judiciary—James Madison's "impenetrable bulwark" against the illegitimate assumption of government power.[27]

That brings us to the granddaddy of all economic liberty cases, *Lochner v. New York*.[28] If unbridled government were a vampire, *Lochner* would be sunlight, holy water, a crucifix, and garlic all rolled into one. Little wonder it is scorned by the establishment and taught to law students as one of the worst Supreme Court decisions of all time. And for people with great faith in the political process—those who believe that government rarely acts for improper purposes like suppressing competition for the benefit of entrenched interests—*Lochner* may well be anathema. But those of us who see government differently tend to see *Lochner* differently as well. We admire its candor.

Lochner involved an 1895 law called the "Bakeshop Act," which prohibited New Yorkers from working in a bakery more than ten hours in one day or sixty hours per week. Like the laundry ordinance in *Yick Wo* and the cigar-making law in *Jacobs*, the Bakeshop Act was presented as a public health measure, designed to protect workers by limiting their exposure to hot, dusty bakeries, and at the same time improve the quality of their products by providing more sanitary and humane working conditions. As in *Yick Wo* and *Jacobs*, however, there were reasons to doubt the veracity of those representations.

Much like the cigar-making law's suspiciously limited geographic coverage, the Bakeshop Act contained numerous exceptions. It did not apply, for example, to bakers who worked in pie bakeries, hotel and restaurant kitchens, clubs, boarding houses, or for private families—even though working conditions in those settings might well be worse than in many of the bakeries covered by the law.[29] Moreover, as Professor Bernstein argues in his meticulously researched book *Rehabilitating Lochner*, the Bakeshop Act's maximum-hours provision was the product of a zealous lobbying effort on the part of unionized bakers who were mostly employed by large commercial bakeries where ten-hour workdays were the norm. Many of them resented competition from immigrant bakers who were accustomed to working longer hours, and whom the union's newspaper called "'the cheap labor of the green hand from foreign shores.'"[30] According to Professor Bernstein, owners of large commercial bakeries also supported the law and "were happy to have the new rules and associated costs and inconveniences imposed on their competitors," the immigrant bakers.[31]

In what may well have been a deliberate test case, the Bakeshop Act was challenged by a German-born baker, Joseph Lochner, who had been arrested twice for allowing employees to work longer hours than the law permitted. The second time he was arrested, Lochner admitted violating the law but claimed it was unconstitutional. The trial judge rejected that argument, and Lochner was convicted. He appealed and lost through every level of the state court system. Believing it would be futile to seek review in the U.S. Supreme Court, his lawyer quit and was replaced by attorney Frank Harvey Field and an unlikely advocate named Henry Weismann.[32]

Weismann was an unlikely advocate for the constitutional challenge to the Bakeshop Act because he had been instrumental in getting the maximum-hours law passed while working as a professional organizer for the bakers' union ten years before. He later quit amid allegations of corruption and opened his own bakery. He also enrolled in Brooklyn Law School, where he was valedictorian of his graduating class of 1903. Just two years later, with his law degree in hand and fresh perspective as a bakery owner and employer, Weismann found himself in the U.S. Supreme Court challenging the very law he had worked so hard to enact.[33]

Given the state of the law at the time, there was no telling how the case would turn out. The Supreme Court had approved a Massachusetts compulsory-vaccination law just days before, and it had upheld a maximum-hours law for miners in Utah a few years earlier.[34] Modern caricatures to the contrary, the Court was no bastion of laissez-faire ideologues.

But the Supreme Court in 1905 did consider occupational freedom a significant constitutional right entitled to meaningful judicial review, so the justices sought to determine the "real object" of New York's maximum-hours law.[35] There were only two possibilities. Either the state was genuinely trying to protect the health of bakers and the public, or it was sandbagging independent bakers in order to prevent them from competing with established firms and the members of the politically influential bakers' union.

Reviewing the record and the parties' arguments, five justices concluded that the state was not plausibly pursuing a legitimate public purpose and voted to strike down the maximum-hours law. Citing the Chinese laundry case, *Yick Wo*, the majority explained that "many of the laws of this character, while passed under what is claimed to be the police power for the purpose of protecting the public health or welfare, are, in reality, passed from other motives."[36] The majority also emphasized that it was not "substituting the judgment of the court for that of the legislature." Instead, it was only deciding whether New York's maximum-hours law was "within the police power of the state."[37] Protecting public health and safety is clearly within the police power, but suppressing competition on behalf of entrenched interests is not. The state failed to persuade the majority that it was genuinely trying to protect the public, just as San Francisco had failed to convince the Court that it was genuinely trying to protect the public from combustible laundries.

Three justices voted to uphold the law as a health measure. Writing for himself and two others, Justice John Marshall Harlan agreed with the proposition that government may not "unduly interfere with the right of the citizen to enter into contracts" or to "earn his livelihood by any lawful calling."[38] But he emphasized that legislatures are vested with "a large discretion" and argued that courts should not overturn a law unless "it be, *beyond question*, plainly and palpably in excess of legislative power."[39] All doubts must be resolved in favor of upholding the law, and "the burden of proof . . . is upon those who assert it to be unconstitutional."[40]

Justice Harlan cited a number of authorities in support of the undisputed proposition that it can be unhealthy for laborers to work long hours. Among his authorities was one Professor Hirt, whose treatise on the "Diseases of Workers" argued that the intense heat in bakeries "induces the workers to resort to cooling drinks," which, together with their tendency to go outside to cool off, "is another source of a number of diseases of various organs."[41]

There was no disagreement between the majority and the Harlan dissent about the legitimacy of courts reviewing government regulations, including economic ones. The disagreement was over how searching that review should be and whether the burden should be on the government to demonstrate that the law serves a legitimate end or on the challenger to prove that it does not.

In a solo dissent, Justice Oliver Wendell Holmes Jr. wrote a paean to judicial restraint that would become one of the most famous opinions in Supreme Court history. Holmes begins his opinion with the remarkable claim that "[t]his case is decided upon an economic theory which a large part of the country does not entertain."[42] Let that soak in for a moment. The "economic theory" to which he's referring is market capitalism—the cornerstone of our society, engine of American prosperity for two centuries, and the only possible system for a country that calls itself "free." But no, says Holmes, "a constitution is not intended to embody a particular economic theory, whether of paternalism . . . or of *laissez faire*. It is made for people of fundamentally differing views."[43] Holmes concludes by saying, "I think that the word liberty in the Fourteenth Amendment is perverted when it is held to prevent the natural outcome of a dominant opinion," unless a reasonable person would necessarily agree that the law in question "would infringe fundamental principles as they have been understood by the traditions of our people and our law."[44]

The three different perspectives on judging reflected in the majority and two dissenting *Lochner* opinions are all featured in modern constitutional law. As explained at the beginning of this chapter, the Supreme Court divides the Constitution's government-limiting provisions into two basic categories: important (fundamental) and unimportant (nonfundamental). Judges apply important constitutional provisions much like the majority did in *Lochner*: they seek to identify the government's true end, ensure that it is constitutionally permissible, and require an appropriate fit between the government's end and the means chosen to advance it. But when dealing with provisions the Supreme Court deems unimportant, judges do none of those things. Indeed, not only will they accept plainly disingenuous explanations for the government's conduct, they will even serve as courtroom advocates when necessary by helping invent justifications for the government's actions. This particularly virulent strain of judicial abdication is called the "rational basis test," and it combines the doe-eyed credulousness of Justice Harlan's dissent in *Lochner* with Holmes's naked hostility to judicial review.

CHAPTER 3

The Rationalize-a-Basis Test

Rational basis review is the distilled essence of judicial abdication. Indeed, when debating judicial engagement, I sometimes call the rational basis test a fraud just to see whether anyone will challenge me on it. So far, no one has. On the contrary, it seems to be an open secret among scholars and practitioners that rational basis review is a sham, but one that has become so ingrained that it would be embarrassing to admit it after all these years.[1] That's deeply troubling because courts use the rational basis test to decide cases all the time. In reality, it's not a test at all but a constitutional shell game in which liberty is the pea that disappears at the end.

I explained in Chapter 2 how the Supreme Court divides rights into two categories, fundamental and nonfundamental. Fundamental rights get meaningful judicial protection; nonfundamental rights get the opposite of that, which is rational basis review.

There are actually two subcategories of meaningful judicial review, which are referred to as "strict" and "intermediate" scrutiny. Strict scrutiny is the most rigorous, as its name implies, and to satisfy that standard the government must show it has a "compelling" interest in addressing a particular problem, for which it has devised a "narrowly tailored" solution that sweeps no more broadly than necessary. Intermediate scrutiny is somewhat less rigorous and is used to protect rights that are considered less significant, but still meaningful, such as commercial speech. Instead of "compelling," the government interest need only be "important"; and instead of being "narrowly tailored," the proposed solution only has to be "closely drawn" or "substantially related" to the problem at hand. These two standards of review, "strict" and "intermediate," are sometimes lumped together under the label "heightened scrutiny," where "heightened" essentially means genuine.

The rational basis test is much different. Unlike strict and intermediate scrutiny, it does not involve a search for truth but rather an exercise in creativity. Instead of trying to determine what the government is *really* up to, as they do in other cases, judges applying rational basis review are required to accept—and even help invent—purely imaginary explanations for the government's actions. You could think of it this way: As a boss, a spouse, or a parent, you sometimes just don't want to know what's really going on. Something seems fishy but you'd rather pretend everything's on the up-and-up because otherwise you might have to do something you'd rather not: discipline an employee, provoke an argument, or punish a child. And that's what the rational basis test often is for judges—a way to pretend the government is acting legitimately when a more searching inquiry would likely show otherwise. Here's how it works.

When the government interferes with rights deemed "nonfundamental" by the Supreme Court (which, again, is most of them), it is not required to justify or even explain its actions. Instead, courts applying rational basis review will presume that the government is acting constitutionally unless the citizen can negate *every conceivable justification* for the government's action—even purely hypothetical ones. Thus, as the Supreme Court has explained, judges applying rational basis review "never require a legislature to articulate its reasons for enacting a statute" and will uphold a law "if there is any reasonably conceivable state of facts that could provide a rational basis" for it.[2] "[T]he existence of facts supporting the legislative judgment is to be presumed,"[3] which means the government "has no obligation to produce evidence, or empirical data to sustain the rationality" of its conduct, and "can base its statutes on rational speculation."[4] Moreover, it is "entirely irrelevant" whether the asserted justification for a law "actually motivated the legislature."[5] Thus, the *actual* motivations of the enacting governmental body are entirely irrelevant," which means that courts must even disregard credible evidence of improper government motives.[6] A law challenged under rational basis review bears a "strong presumption" of validity, and those challenging the law must "negative every conceivable basis which might support it."[7] Finally, judges are not merely permitted but *"obligated* to seek out other conceivable reasons for validating" a challenged law if the government is unable to invent a sufficiently persuasive justification for its own policy.[8]

Does that sound like real judging to you? Let's go through the rational basis test step by step.

1. *It is "entirely irrelevant" whether the asserted justification actually motivated the legislature.*

This means the government is permitted to mislead the court regarding its true ends by offering purely pretextual explanations as support for the challenged law. Compare this with "heightened" scrutiny, where judges believe they can not only determine the government's true ends but also distinguish between ends that are "compelling" and those that are merely "important." Indeed, when deciding cases involving fundamental rights, judges seem confident in their ability to see through legislative smokescreens and identify the government's actual ends, even when the government tries to conceal them, as it sometimes does.[9] For example, the Supreme Court has explained that while it is "normally deferential to a State's articulation of a secular purpose" in establishment clause challenges, it nevertheless insists that the "statement of such purpose be sincere and not a sham."[10] Similarly, in rejecting the state's exclusion of women from the Virginia Military Institute, the Court explained that the government must provide a "genuine" explanation for its actions, and not one that has been "hypothesized or invented *post hoc* in response to litigation."[11]

So when courts refuse to determine the government's true end in rational basis cases, it's not because they are unable to do so—it's because the Supreme Court has decided they shouldn't even bother to try.

2. *Those challenging a law must negate every conceivable justification for it.* This is absurd. It is hard enough (some would say impossible, though that appears to be incorrect as a matter of formal logic) to prove a specific negative, but proving an infinite set of negatives, including purely hypothetical ones? Preposterous. After all, there might still be dinosaurs in some remote corner of the world, and there are certainly species of plants that no one has discovered yet. Maybe that's why Louisiana licenses florists—so they can protect us from a potentially deadly new species of daffodil. If a government lawyer is prepared to assert that with a straight face, who's to say it's inconceivable? Because the rational basis test is more about imagination than facts, it is actually quite challenging to negate all "conceivable" justifications for a law. I used to use radioactive space monkeys as an example of something so preposterous as to exceed even the most whimsical application of rational basis review, but I had to abandon that illustration when I found out that NASA actually has a radioactive monkey program.[12]

Notably, courts seem to understand perfectly well how unrealistic the prove-a-negative requirement is when the shoe is on the other foot. Thus, when a defendant tried to exclude a recorded conversation from a trial because the government had failed to prove the recording was not made for a "criminal, tortious or other injurious purpose," a federal appellate court rejected that effort because otherwise the government would face "an impossible burden of proving three negatives."[13] What a remarkable double standard. Citizens trying to vindicate their constitutional rights must negate an *infinite* set of hypothetical justifications, whereas the government, in trying to convict someone of a crime, cannot be expected to negate just three specific propositions because it would be "impossible" to do so. Talk about a stacked deck.

3. Judges are "obligated" to come up with other justifications for a law besides those offered by the government.

In regular English: Judges are required to help the government win rational basis cases by abandoning judicial neutrality and serving as courtroom advocates for one party in a legal dispute. That would be an outrage in any other setting, and a clear violation of judicial ethics.[14] But in Rational Basis Land, it's just another day at the courthouse.

Imagine you're a lawyer trying your first case. It's a breach-of-contract case against the government, and on the first day of trial, the judge calls the lawyers to the bench and says, "Before we begin, I need to disclose that I have been retained by the government's lawyers to help them think of possible defenses to the breach-of-contract claim. I want to emphasize that I will not assist the government in any other way, nor will I actually help think up possible justifications for the government's conduct unless necessary to help the government win its case."

It would be malpractice for a lawyer to proceed to trial under those circumstances because due process requires a neutral adjudicator. A judge who is obligated to help one party prevail in a lawsuit simply because of that party's status—be it government, corporation, nonprofit, employer, employee, etc.—is not neutral. But that is precisely the role that judges play in rational basis cases. How on earth could that seem fair to anyone? One answer is that it really doesn't matter whether judges are neutral in rational basis cases because they are not serving a genuinely adjudicative function. Instead, their role is to provide the appearance of judicial review without determining what the government is really up to or requiring an honest (and potentially embarrassing) account of its actions.

That this is considered an appropriate methodology in the legal field came as quite a surprise to my nonlawyer colleague Dick Carpenter, a university professor with a Ph.D. in research methodology. As I sat in his office one day explaining the mechanics of rational basis review, Dick's expression grew steadily more quizzical until he finally stopped me and said, "Wait a minute—do they teach it that way in law school?" I said yes, that's how the rational basis test works and that's how it's taught: the government's true end is irrelevant; it need not support its factual assertions with evidence; and judges must invent justifications for the government's actions if necessary to uphold the law. "And no one questions that?" Self-conscious pause. "Not really, no."

But we really should. Think what it would look like if other people did their jobs that way. If, say, a meat inspector were acting like a judge in a constitutional case, he'd first have to ask what kind of meat it was in order to know how carefully to inspect it. If it's beef—call it a "fundamental" food group—the inspector will make a serious effort to determine whether the meat is unwholesome. He'll check the bacteria count and give the meat a good sniff and a careful visual inspection. But if it's a "nonfundamental" food like chicken or pork, he'll just assume the meat is good and give it a quick once-over while holding his breath to avoid smelling it. No bacteria check, no serious effort to determine whether the meat is in fact rotten or wholesome.

And how about rational basis parenting?

Kid pulls into the driveway after curfew. Rational basis father steps into the garage.

"Lexi, dear, where might you have been this evening?"

"Sorry, dad—I know I'm late. Julie's parents are out of town, so she had this wild party and . . ."

"Whoa there, young lady. I didn't say where *were* you, I said where *might* you have been?"

"Oh, OK." Pause. "I guess maybe I was at the, uh . . ."—encouraging nod—"nursing home?"—nod—". . . reading books to old people?"

"Oh, the nursing home. That's so sweet of you."

Car door opens, beer can falls out. Awkward silence.

"And where might that beer can have come from?"

"Well, I gave some friends a ride home and they had a case of beer back there."

"Let's try again. I said where *might* that beer have come from?"

"Oh, right—sorry. Well, I gave some friends a ride home from the part-, I mean the nursing home, and they were in the back seat, and they were, um . . . they were kind of, uh . . . Oh geez, I don't know, Dad, I'm really struggling with this one—can you help me out?"

"Well, maybe you guys went out and collected empty cans so you could use the deposits to buy some new books for the nursing home. And you just forgot to turn that one in."

"Oh, yeah—that could totally be where it came from."

"You're such a sweet kid, Lexi. Always helping other people and never doing anything wrong."

"Aww, thanks, Rational Basis Dad. I love you the most!"

Besides displaying a sometimes stunning credulity about the political process, judges in rational basis cases frequently emphasize that courts do not sit as a "superlegislature" to "weigh the wisdom of legislation."[15] But this presumes that laws consistently reflect the "wisdom" of policymakers, which they do not. In reality, many laws are the product of ignorance, animus, favoritism, cronyism, logrolling, and myriad other impulses that have nothing whatever to do with legislative "wisdom." It is dangerous and naïve to suppose otherwise.

Proponents of judicial deference take comfort in the unfounded belief that legislative acts reliably reflect the will of the public. That may be appealing in principle, but such faith in the political process ignores the realities of governmental institutions. Through gerrymandering and other means, elected representatives are increasingly insulated from their constituents. Meanwhile, many policies and regulations are set and enforced by unelected, unaccountable agencies and commissions. What's more, some members of Congress lack the competence, interest, or motivation to learn whether their acts are constitutional. They are elected, and reelected, for delivering goods to their constituents, not for telling constituents "no" because the Constitution forbids it.

Paradoxically, conservatives who rail against the so-called living Constitution are often the most ardent proponents of rational basis judicial deference. Yet under both doctrines, the Constitution means whatever the politicians say it means, and judging becomes politics by another name. A key function of rational basis review is to enable judges to avoid the responsibility of confronting the other branches in those areas, such as the economic sphere, where courts no longer wish to fulfill their role as an independent check on government power. The following three cases, one from each level of the federal judiciary, illustrate that point.

The dairy industry has a long history of interest-group politics, special pleading, and naked economic protectionism. So it is perhaps fitting that the Supreme Court formalized the doctrine of judicial abdication in a milk-related case called *United States v. Carolene Products Co.*[16] Decided in 1938, the issue in *Carolene Products* was the constitutionality of a federal law banning the shipment of "filled milk." Filled milk is skim milk to which vegetable oil has been added to replace the missing butterfat. Led by dairy producers, supporters of the ban claimed that filled milk was unhealthy and amounted to a fraud on the public. Congress held hearings and, using materials submitted by the law's proponents, constructed a legislative "record" filled with innuendo, junk science, and outright fabrications to support those patently false claims.[17] The filled-milk ban was, as Professor Geoffrey Miller explained in a seminal article, "an utterly unprincipled example of special interest legislation."[18]

But the Supreme Court by 1938 was already well along in its campaign to avoid meaningful scrutiny of economic regulations. *Carolene Products* was the case in which the Court finally articulated a theory for the rubber-stamp style of judging that would come to be known as rational basis review. The famous "Footnote Four" of *Carolene Products* is where the Supreme Court formalized the distinction between important and unimportant constitutional rights. According to Footnote Four, important rights are most of the ones specifically listed in the Constitution, along with rights affecting one's ability to participate in the political process and the right of "discrete and insular minorities" not to be discriminated against.[19] Whereas those rights may be restricted only for good reason, the rights deemed unimportant—such as the ability to buy and sell ordinary consumer goods or run a business—may be regulated for virtually any reason on the basis of purely hypothetical concerns. In these cases, "the existence of facts supporting the legislative judgment is to be presumed" and an economic regulation will not be struck down unless "it is of such a character as to *preclude the assumption* that it rests upon some rational basis within the knowledge and experience of the legislators."[20]

But allowing courts to base their rulings on imaginary facts and hypothetical rationales throws the door open for mischief, as vividly illustrated by the *Carolene Products* case itself. Commenting on the majority opinion that upheld the filled-milk ban, Professor Miller remarked that the "purported 'public interest' justifications so credulously reported" were so "patently bogus" that it was "difficult to believe that members of the Court were unaware of the true motivation behind the legislation."[21] Instead, the justices simply decided it was no longer their job to ensure that the government was pursuing constitutionally legitimate ends in the economic sphere or employing constitutionally permissible means to achieve them.

The Supreme Court followed *Carolene Products* with a series of decisions upholding nakedly anticompetitive regulations on everything from fitting eyeglass frames[22] to debt adjusting,[23] and even a Louisiana law that allowed existing river pilots to fill new job openings with their friends and family members, effectively closing the occupation to perfectly qualified outsiders.[24] The message was clear: from now on, courts will give legislatures a free pass in the economic sphere. And boy, did the lower courts get the message.

It would be impossible to list all the instances of judicial abdication by lower courts that have rubber-stamped nakedly anticompetitive economic regulations, but two occupational licensing cases litigated by the Institute for Justice provide a representative sample.

Case No. 1: Florida is one of just three states in the country that require a license to practice interior design. In order to get a license, would-be designers must have a college degree from an accredited interior design school; they must serve a two-year apprenticeship with a state-licensed interior designer; and they must pass a three-day, thousand-dollar licensing exam administered by a private testing body. The true purpose of Florida's interior design law is perfectly clear: it is to increase wages for state-licensed interior designers by limiting the supply of labor and closing off jobs in Florida to designers from other states.[25] Indeed, the legislative history confirms that the law was drafted by, lobbied for, and passed at the behest of industry members who did not provide even a shred of evidence to support their claim that unlicensed interior design presents a safety risk. More than a dozen state studies have confirmed the absence of any harm to the public from unlicensed interior design, which is the norm in this country since forty-seven states do not license interior designers.[26] And when Florida's interior design law was challenged in court by the Institute for Justice on behalf of three aspiring interior designers, the state stipulated it had no evidence that unlicensed practice presents any genuine public welfare concerns or that the licensing of interior designers has benefited the public in any way.[27]

Despite no evidence of public benefit and a mountain of evidence showing the interior design law's true anticompetitive purpose, a federal trial judge upheld the law on the surmise that it might genuinely have been "intended to protect public safety . . . or . . . consumers from incompetent or poorly trained interior designers."[28] The sole support for these findings was a twenty-two-year-old committee report that incorporated verbatim the unsubstantiated claims of the interest groups that drafted and lobbied for the law.[29] The court of appeals was even more credulous in affirming the decision, accepting at face value statutory boilerplate to the effect that "the Florida legislature was primarily concerned with protecting Florida consumers from safety risks." In its decision upholding the law, the appellate court studiously avoided any citation to the evidentiary record, which made clear that the purported safety concerns were entirely illusory and the only plausible purpose of the law was to suppress competition.

Case No. 2: As noted in the Introduction, Louisiana is the only state in the country that requires a license to sell floral arrangements. At the time the licensing law was challenged in court, in 2003, applicants had to pass a highly subjective practical exam in which they had four hours to create four floral arrangements that would be judged on such points as whether the flowers were picked properly and whether the arrangement had the correct "focal point." These judgments were made not by a theoretically disinterested bureaucrat, but by working florists with an obvious financial incentive to minimize the number of state-licensed florists. Not surprisingly, the pass rate on the florist exam was low—just 36 percent. By way of comparison, the pass rate on the Louisiana bar exam was 61.5 percent.[30] The specific requirements have since been changed, but a license is still necessary to work as a florist. Does it really seem plausible that the citizens of Louisiana, alone among the states, need government to protect them from the ravages of unlicensed floristry?

A federal trial court judge thought so. In a decision upholding the law under rational basis review in 2005, the judge acknowledged that people have a constitutional right to pursue the "common occupations of life" subject to "reasonable limitations," but then upheld the law as an appropriate effort on the legislature's part to enhance the reputation of Louisiana's floral industry and protect consumers from the physical dangers of unlicensed floristry. According to the judge, those dangers included exposed floral picks, broken floral wire, and "infect[ed] dirt."[31] The only "evidence" cited for this proposition was the testimony of the Louisiana Horticulture Commission's chief enforcement officer, who was unable to identify even a single injury in any of the forty-nine states that do not license florists. Nor was there any evidence that Louisiana's licensing scheme had done anything to "enhance" the state's floral industry, as later confirmed by an Institute for Justice study in which working florists from Texas and Louisiana were asked to judge the quality of floral arrangements from randomly selected shops in both states. The florists found no difference between the arrangements from Texas and those from Louisiana.[32]

The essential credulousness of rational basis review was on full display in the court's decision upholding the florist licensing law. Among other things, there is no mention in the judge's opinion that the lead defendant in the case, the agriculture commissioner Bob Odom, admitted that he had promised the Louisiana State Florists' Association whatever they wanted by way of licensing. This included killing a deregulation bill in the Louisiana senate's agriculture committee after it had passed the state house of representatives by a vote of 92 to 3.[33] Like many occupational licensing laws, Louisiana's florist licensing scheme was passed for one reason and one reason only: to shield politically connected industry members from fair competition.

Predictably, the courts' withdrawal from providing any meaningful judicial review of economic regulations invited a special-interest feeding frenzy that continues to this day. Judicial abdication has allowed the American Dream to become ensnared in a net of government red tape that is gradually strangling the nation's entrepreneurial spirit. How bad is it? Consider:

- In the 1950s, just 5 percent of the American workforce was subject to occupational licensing. Today, that number is 30 percent.[34]
- Occupational licensing costs the national economy about $100 billion per year in lost output. On top of that, there is also about $300 billion redistributed every year from consumers to members of licensed occupations.[35]
- Licensing requirements vary wildly from state to state and from occupation to occupation. For example, ten states require four months or more of training for manicurists, whereas Alaska demands only about three days and Iowa about nine days. The average length of training required for emergency medical technicians is 33 days; for cosmetologists it is 372 days.
- Occupational licensing has either no impact or even a negative impact on the quality of services provided to customers by members of the regulated occupation.[36]

- Studies have shown that occupational licensing can actually harm people by driving up the prices charged by regulated occupations, such as electricians, to the point where consumers try to do the work themselves—sometimes with tragic results.[37]

The assault on competition, innovation, and economic liberty by special interests is relentless.[38] No occupation is too obscure, no product too harmless, no service too innocent that some legislator will not try to regulate it in the name of public safety or consumer protection. But it is no use looking to the courts to protect our economic liberty as we do with other liberties like speech and religion, because make-believe judging is no protection against government misbehavior.

Finally, no discussion of the rational basis test would be complete without noting the inconsistent way the Supreme Court has applied it and the perception that there are actually two versions of the test: one with "bite" and one without.[39] Practically speaking, this means that in some cases the government will be given a "free pass" to pursue constitutionally illegitimate ends and in some cases it will not.[40] In some cases, the government's inability to support its factual assertions with evidence will matter; in other cases it will not. To put it in the simplest terms, some rational basis cases involve a genuine search for the truth, but most do not.

The turn-a-blind-eye approach is epitomized in what has become the Supreme Court's most influential economic liberty case, *Williamson v. Lee Optical of Oklahoma, Inc.* (1955),[41] involving an Oklahoma law that prohibited opticians from duplicating lenses or putting old lenses into new frames without a prescription from an eye doctor. As the lower court found, opticians are perfectly capable of duplicating and fitting lenses without a prescription, and they do so all the time. Based on a careful review of the evidence, the court concluded that the legislature had "arbitrarily" legislated opticians "out of a long recognized trade."[42] The Supreme Court reversed and offered a series of surmises about what the legislature "might have concluded" about the supposed benefits of requiring people to visit an eye doctor for something as mundane as a change of frames.[43] But there was no actual evidence to support those hypotheses because the Court was making them up out of thin air. Notably missing from the Court's opinion is any consideration of the possibility that the sole purpose of those restrictions might very well have been—and almost certainly was—to favor one group at the expense of another.

But other times, the Supreme Court refuses to make up justifications for the government's actions in rational basis cases and refuses to accept justifications that the government has obviously invented after the fact, as it normally would do. Among the clearest examples is *City of Cleburne v. Cleburne Living Center* (1985),[44] in which the Court found unconstitutional a city's refusal to grant a permit to a group home for mentally retarded adults. Though clearly motivated by irrational prejudice, the city invented a number of post hoc justifications for denying the permit, including the fact that the home was to be located in a five-hundred-year flood plain from which residents might not be able to escape should the need arise, and also that students at a nearby junior high school might harass the residents of the home.[45] But the Court rejected those explanations and noted that they were unsupported in the record.[46]

Normally, the government is allowed to make up explanations for its conduct in rational basis cases, and the fact that it has no evidence to support those explanations—or indeed, that they are not even true—is typically not a problem. As Justice Marshall noted in his separate opinion, the City of Cleburne's disingenuous explanations for its conduct "surely would be valid under the traditional rational-basis test applicable to economic and commercial regulation."[47] But the Court was not applying exactly the same standard in this case, Marshall explained: "however labeled, the rational-basis test invoked today is most assuredly not the rational-basis test of *Williamson v. Lee Optical of Oklahoma, Inc.*"[48]

The idea that there are significantly different versions of the rational basis test persists to this day. In the same-sex marriage cases that were argued in March 2013, for instance, Solicitor General Donald Verrilli argued that the only way for the Court to uphold federal and state restrictions on gay marriage would be to apply an essentially content-free standard of review that he referred to variously as "Lee Optical rational basis review" and "the minimal rationality standard of Lee Optical." Thus, he assumed that another kind of rational basis review exists.[49] Justice Ginsburg also made that point when she challenged the idea that "if you get into rational basis, then it's anything goes." She referred to a 1971 case, *Reed v. Reed*, in which "the Court did something it had never done in the history of the country under rational basis": it concluded that a law involved "rank discrimination" and struck it down on that basis.[50] Her point seemed to be that the *Reed* Court did not give the government a free pass, as it typically would under rational basis review and as it is widely perceived to have done in *Williamson v. Lee Optical*.

Whether the Supreme Court has adopted two versions of the rational basis test or instead applies the same test with varying degrees of rigor, the fact is that courts applying rational basis review sometimes try to determine the actual reasons for the government's actions but usually do not. I believe that is the real difference between "rational basis with bite" or "rational basis plus" (or any other form of so-called "heightened scrutiny") on the one hand, and plain old rational basis review or what the solicitor general called "Lee Optical rational basis review" on the other: the former involve a genuine effort to ensure that the government is pursuing a constitutionally permissible end; the latter do not.[51] If this is not a fair assessment, then it seems to me it is high time for the Supreme Court to clarify that there is only one rational basis test and that it is always a search for truth. That has certainly not been the case in the past, and the Court's failure to make such a clarification grows more deafening with each new rational basis decision it hands down.

CHAPTER 4

A Watered-Down
Constitution

The mentality that allows courts to abandon their customary truth-seeking function and invent baseless justifications for government conduct in rational basis cases is unfortunately present in other settings as well. It is the nature of government to keep pushing the limits of its authority. Regrettably, the courts have acquiesced in many areas of law. Sometimes they do it gradually and sometimes suddenly, but the general trend in many areas has been to keep giving the government more leeway until it is committing precisely the abuses that a particular constitutional provision was designed to prevent. This chapter explores that trend through the lens of cases involving eminent domain abuse, the abrogation of loan agreements in violation of the contract clause, the demise of enumerated powers as a significant check on the federal government, and the judiciary's extreme reluctance to protect unenumerated rights, even when people's lives are endangered by unaccountable bureaucrats.

BULLDOZING PROPERTY RIGHTS—THE *KELO* TRAVESTY
In May 2005, a Texas businessman was finalizing a deal to build a high-tech manufacturing plant in Jiangsu province, China. His host took him to the future site of the plant, where there was a small village.

Asked how they could build a factory there, the host explained that the government would make the villagers leave. To which the American confidently (and perhaps a little proudly) replied, "You can't do that in my country."[1] Turns out he was wrong. Just one month later, the U.S. Supreme Court decided a case, *Kelo v. City of New London*,[2] in which it approved the use of eminent domain to transfer property from one private owner to another, just like the Chinese government did to make way for the factory in Jiangsu.

Americans were stunned, then outraged. Polls show that *Kelo* is one of the most reviled Supreme Court decisions in history, and for good reason. It is among the most glaring examples of judicial abdication since the New Deal, and it meant that every home and every small business was at risk of being gobbled up by land-hungry developers and tax-hungry politicians like the New London city council.

Kelo was a wakeup call for many Americans, a warning that the Supreme Court's understanding of the Constitution and the legitimate prerogatives of government is much different from their own. It is impossible to appreciate how desperate the need is for a fully engaged judiciary without understanding the extent to which abdication has become a central operating principle for America's courts. *Kelo* drove that point home in a way most Americans found both alarming and repugnant.

The *Kelo* saga began in 1997, when the City of New London, Connecticut, hatched a plan to revive its flagging economy by bulldozing the working-class neighborhood of Fort Trumbull and turning the land over to a property developer who promised to transform it into an upscale suburban enclave, complete with a river walk, new office space, four-star hotel, and high-end housing for employees of Pfizer's nearby global research facility. The idea originated with a self-styled visionary named Claire Gaudiani, who was president of New London's Connecticut College and also head of the New London Development Corporation. It happened that Gaudiani's husband was a high-ranking Pfizer executive, and she knew Pfizer was considering expanding its operations on the East Coast. So she proposed redeveloping the Fort Trumbull neighborhood to Pfizer's "requirements"—and using eminent domain to take by force whatever property the city couldn't acquire through voluntary means.[3]

When questioned about the propriety of using eminent domain to oust people like eighty-one-year-old Wilhelmina Dery, who was born in her house at 87 Walbach Street and lived there her entire life, Gaudiani replied, "Anything that's working in our great nation is working because somebody left skin on the sidewalk."[4]

Some Fort Trumbull residents refused to sell; they wanted to stay in their homes and live in the new development. But city officials were adamant, and on the day before Thanksgiving 2000 they began sending condemnation notices advising remaining residents that if they refused to sell voluntarily, the city would use eminent domain to seize their properties. The city's message was clear: You're leaving—no ifs, ands, or buts. The residents' response was equally clear: Hell no, these homes belong to us.

Represented by lawyers from the Institute for Justice and led by a soft-spoken but iron-willed nurse named Susette Kelo, the Fort Trumbull property owners took their case all the way to the U.S. Supreme Court. Their argument was simple: the Fifth Amendment says private property may be taken only for a "public use," like a highway or a school. Taking property from one private owner and giving it to another in the hopes that the new owner will build a more expensive home or a more profitable business is not a public use and therefore not allowed.

The city's lawyers argued for a sweeping interpretation of the Fifth Amendment in which the words "public use" would be replaced with "public purpose." Justice O'Connor exposed the implications of that position when she asked whether it meant the government could take a Motel 6 using eminent domain and give the property to a Ritz-Carlton simply because a nicer hotel would generate more taxes. The city's lawyer responded: "Yes, your Honor. That would be okay."[5] A few months later, five justices of the Supreme Court agreed. But Justice O'Connor—and the vast majority of Americans—did not.

No Supreme Court decision in living memory has provoked a more passionate, more intense, or more nearly unanimous public backlash than *Kelo*. Polling has consistently recorded overwhelming opposition to the decision, and politicians from across the ideological spectrum were quick to disavow it. The decision seemed self-evidently wrong to most Americans, who until that point had been blissfully unaware that the Supreme Court relegated property rights to nonfundamental status decades ago. There is much to criticize in the *Kelo* decision, and it is well worth comparing Justice Stevens's government-empowering majority opinion with the dissents by Justice O'Connor and Justice Thomas. Three aspects of the decision stand out particularly.

First, it is profoundly un-American. Throughout history and in most of the world today, governments have degraded property rights, either denying them outright or brushing them aside as convenience dictates. Most people believe that America was supposed to be different, that law-abiding citizens own their homes and businesses not at the sufferance of government officials but as a matter of *right*. The sanctity of private property is a key element of America's self-perception as "the land of the free"—and *Kelo* broke faith with it.

Second, *Kelo* watered down the Fifth Amendment's public-use provision to the point where it is functionally meaningless. Among the bedrock principles of American constitutional law, as laid down by the Supreme Court in 1798, is that it "cannot be considered a rightful exercise of legislative authority" when the government "takes property from A. and gives it to B."[6] The *Kelo* majority effectively repudiated that principle by tacking on the qualifier ". . . unless the government thinks B might make more money with it." As Justice O'Connor pointed out in her dissent, after *Kelo* "the specter of condemnation hangs over all property. Nothing is to prevent the State from replacing any Motel 6 with a Ritz-Carlton, any home with a shopping mall, or any farm with a factory."[7] But that is precisely what the public-use requirement was designed to prevent, and the *Kelo* majority stripped that protection from the Constitution with the wave of a pen.

Third, the majority opinion in *Kelo* reflects a remarkably naïve view of policymaking and the way eminent domain is used in real life. In his majority opinion, Justice Stevens presents an image of government officials weighing various options and seeking input from affected property owners while carefully balancing the anticipated benefits to society with the harm inflicted on the dispossessed. Stevens particularly emphasizes the "comprehensive character" of New London's redevelopment plan and the supposedly "thorough deliberation that preceded its adoption."[8]

But that is not how the decision was made to use eminent domain in Fort Trumbull, and it is not how decisions to use eminent domain are typically made. Indeed, evidence presented at the *Kelo* trial showed that the New London Development Corporation relentlessly pursued its demolition plan because Pfizer "[did not] want to be surrounded by tenements." The NLDC's president, Claire Gaudiani, insisted that seizing and destroying the Fort Trumbull homes was the only option available.[9] But experts who reviewed the development plan noted that there were other alternatives, and one architect even crafted an alternative plan that would have preserved the neighborhood instead of demolishing it.[10]

In reality, decisions to use eminent domain are often driven by property developers looking to shortcut the normal process of acquiring properties through voluntary transactions. Put land-hungry developers in a room with tax-hungry politicians and the abuse of eminent domain is practically assured when there is no judicial supervision.[11]

Kelo effectively deleted the "public use" provision from the Fifth Amendment. The decision allows government to treat private property like a public asset to be rearranged at will in the hope of creating jobs, increasing tax revenue, or stimulating the economy. But government has a consistently poor track record in all of these areas, so it should be no surprise that New London's grand plans for Fort Trumbull never materialized. Instead, the property developer dropped out, Pfizer packed up and left New London, and to this day the neighborhood remains a barren, bulldozed wasteland. As documented in a study by IJ's Castle Coalition called *Redevelopment Wrecks*, that is not an uncommon result when government uses eminent domain to take by force what it should have pursued through voluntary agreements with existing property owners.[12]

Kelo was not just a bad decision on the merits; it was the culmination of a campaign to relegate property rights to second-class status. But property is the very essence of freedom: without it there can be no autonomy, no sanctuary, and no space for dissent or creative endeavor. The Constitution protects property rights consistent with that understanding. The Supreme Court does not. That is the very essence of judicial abdication.

JUDICIAL REPEAL OF THE CONTRACT CLAUSE

Most Americans found the Supreme Court's cavalier treatment of property rights in *Kelo* appalling. What they may not have realized is just how easy it is for judges to gut any constitutional right, no matter how clearly expressed. A particularly glaring example involves a constitutional provision that says states may not pass "any Law impairing the Obligation of Contracts."[13] This provision is known as the contract clause, and the Framers considered it so important that it is one of the few express limits on state power to be found in the original Constitution. In a 1934 case called *Home Building & Loan Ass'n v. Blaisdell*, the Supreme Court effectively wiped it away.[14]

The Framers had a particular kind of contractual arrangement in mind when they wrote the contract clause: loans. People who borrow money typically outnumber those who lend it. This creates a risk that borrowers will use the political process to alter or abolish the terms of their loans, especially in an economic downturn. That is precisely what happened in the wake of the Revolutionary War, when many state legislatures passed laws that substantially altered the terms of mortgages and other loan agreements in favor of debtors.[15] While such laws appear humane on their face, they have serious unintended consequences, such as making credit more expensive and difficult to get. Uncertainty equals risk, and risk gets passed on to borrowers in the form of higher interest rates. There is also a moral issue. As Cicero asked more than two thousand years ago, "what is the meaning of an abolition of debts, except that you buy a farm with my money; that you have the farm, and I have not my money?"[16]

It was with those understandings in mind that the Framers decided to include a provision that specifically prohibits states from impairing the obligation of contracts. They were well aware of the harsh results that might sometimes follow from this choice, but they understood too that giving democratic majorities the power to vote their way out of debt would be equally disastrous for the nation's economic well-being and, even more importantly, for the rule of law.

Fast-forward to the Great Depression—Minnesota, 1933. With crushing unemployment and the economy in the tank, many people are having trouble making their loan payments. Banks are foreclosing on farms and homes. In response to public pressure, the Minnesota legislature declares a state of economic emergency and passes a law authorizing local courts to exempt properties from foreclosure for up to two years. For lenders, that's a big deal. The whole point of a mortgage is that the property provides security for the loan, which is why interest rates on mortgages are lower than many other loans. A lender who cannot promptly foreclose on the mortgaged property is being exposed to unbargained-for risk, and that risk will be passed on to future borrowers in the form of higher interest rates and lending costs.

The tendency of political majorities to alter or abolish their debts during "economic emergencies" was the *precise reason* why the Framers included the contract clause in the Constitution. So what would the Supreme Court do when confronted by a state law that was politically popular but specifically prohibited by the contract clause? Abdicate.

In a rambling opinion by Chief Justice Hughes, a 5-4 majority in *Blaisdell* acknowledged that the purpose of the contract clause was to prevent debtors from using the political process to alter the terms of their loans.[17] But Hughes then rationalized his way around the contract clause by questioning whether the two-year foreclosure suspension actually "impaired" the affected loan contracts—even though the state conceded that it did. Either way, he argued, the Minnesota legislature's declaration of an "economic emergency" was one to which the courts should defer, along with the "reasonableness" of the legislative response. This was so, the majority claimed, because "there [had] been a growing appreciation of public needs and of the necessity of finding [common] ground for a rational compromise between individual rights and public welfare."[18] So even though the Framers enshrined private contracts in the text of the original Constitution *for the specific purpose* of preventing laws like Minnesota's foreclosure suspension, five justices of the Supreme Court decided they would not enforce that provision because they believed they knew better.

In a dissent joined by three others, Justice George Sutherland demolished the majority opinion. He began by warning that the Court's failure to hold the line against Minnesota's legislative assault on the Constitution would result in "gradual but ever-advancing encroachments upon the sanctity of private and public contracts."[19] He then showed how the majority's reliance on the Minnesota legislature's declaration of an "economic emergency" got the constitutional reasoning exactly backward. The dissenting opinion meticulously documented how the Framers were well aware that political pressure to alter the obligation of contracts would be most intense during times of economic crisis, and they included the contract clause for the specific purpose of preventing that from happening.[20] As Sutherland explained, this provision "was meant to foreclose state action impairing the obligation of contracts *primarily and especially* in respect of such action aimed at giving relief to debtors *in time of emergency*."[21]

Besides its affront to principles of contract, *Blaisdell* raised an even more troubling issue: If the Supreme Court could not be counted on to enforce a crystal-clear restriction like the contract clause, was there any hope for judicial enforcement of less precise—but even more momentous—constitutional limits like the doctrine of enumerated federal powers? As the nation soon discovered, the answer was no. The Supreme Court had eaten from the tree of judicial abdication, and it liked the taste.

FAREWELL TO FEDERALISM

Recall from Chapter 1 that the Framers believed the Constitution's most important protection for liberty would be the concept of enumerated powers, by which Congress would (at least in theory) be restricted to exercising only those powers actually delegated to it by the people. Founding-era Americans were so concerned about the possibility of exchanging a foreign tyranny for one of their own creation that many of them opposed ratifying the Constitution for that reason alone. But supporters of ratification assured skeptics that the federal government would have such limited powers that it could never pose a serious threat to liberty. After one of the most remarkable political debates in human history, Americans were finally persuaded. As a result, the promise of limited government became the basis of the constitutional bargain struck when the Constitution was ratified in 1788. Americans were specifically assured that the powers of the federal government would be "few and defined." And they believed it.

That promise was largely kept for a century and a half. But in the midst of the Great Depression, Congress and the president sought to revoke it by imposing a system of top-down management and central planning on the national economy. Members of President Roosevelt's "Brain Trust" thought they knew better than the Framers how much government America needed, and they had little regard for outdated notions of federal power. As a leading member of the Brain Trust named Rexford Tugwell later acknowledged, squaring New Deal policies with the Constitution required "tortured interpretations of a document intended to prevent them."[22]

At first, the Court stood firm, striking down a number of laws including the National Industrial Recovery Act, which was designed to reduce "destructive competition" in various industries by fixing prices and wages.[23] The justices struck down these programs not because they disagreed with them as a matter of economic policy (though no doubt some of them did), but because the Constitution in their understanding protects liberty by delegating a finite set of powers to the federal government. In striking down a federal bid to micromanage the coal industry, Justice Sutherland explained that the decision to "preserve complete and unimpaired state self-government" in all matters not committed to the federal government "is one of the plainest facts" that emerges from a study of the Framers' deliberations and those of the state ratifying conventions.[24] Indeed, if there had been any inkling that the states might one day be reduced to "little more than geographical subdivisions of the national domain"—which was precisely the goal of the New Deal legislation—it is safe to say the Constitution "would never have been ratified."[25]

But President Roosevelt made clear that he was prepared to provoke a constitutional crisis if need be in order to bend the Supreme Court to his will. This effort culminated with his infamous court-packing scheme, in which he proposed adding up to six new justices to the Court in order to ensure favorable rulings in future challenges. The scheme met with strong public and legislative disapproval and was never enacted. But there was no need: whether through a loss of will, misplaced fidelity to majoritarian impulses, or a sea change in ideology, the Supreme Court simply stopped making any serious effort to restrict Congress to its constitutionally enumerated powers.

That fact was demonstrated most dramatically in a 1942 case called *Wickard v. Filburn*,[26] involving the constitutionality of a federal law that limited the amount of wheat that farmers could grow on their own land. Nothing in the Constitution gives Congress specific authority to regulate the price or supply of agricultural products, much less tell farmers how much they may produce.[27] The government sought to get around this obstacle, as it typically does, by invoking its enumerated power to regulate interstate commerce. Just one small problem: Roscoe Filburn grew all his wheat for consumption on his own farm in Ohio, and he neither bought nor sold wheat on the interstate market. Thus, in his case, there was no "interstate commerce" to regulate.

But the lack of any *actual* interstate commerce proved no hindrance to the Supreme Court, which was perfectly willing to uphold the law on the basis of *imaginary* interstate commerce using what came to be called the "aggregation principle." In essence, the Court asked what the effect would be of many farmers following Filburn's example and producing all the wheat they needed on their own farms. Naturally, the result would be fewer purchases of wheat, which in turn would have a "substantial effect" on the interstate wheat market. In the Supreme Court's reasoning, the fact that Filburn's "own contribution to the demand for wheat [from the interstate market] may be trivial by itself is not enough to remove him from the scope of federal regulation where, as here, his contribution, taken together with that of many others similarly situated, is far from trivial."[28]

Of course, any activity sufficiently aggregated can be said to have a substantial effect on the national economy. Dental hygiene: the more people brush their teeth, the more toothpaste and toothbrushes the market will need to supply; the less they do it, the more dentists. Reading a book? You either bought that book on the interstate book market or else you borrowed it, in which case you withheld your business from the interstate book market, just like farmer Filburn withheld his business from the interstate wheat market by growing his own. What about just staring off into space—does that affect interstate commerce? Well, you could have been working and contributing to the gross domestic product instead of daydreaming. Or you could have helped stimulate the economy by going shopping. Or eating bacon that had moved, deliciously, in interstate commerce.

That the Supreme Court has utterly abandoned any serious commitment to holding the federal government to its constitutionally authorized powers was made clear by a 2005 case involving medical marijuana called *Gonzales v. Raich*,[29] and the 2012 blockbuster, *National Federation of Independent Business v. Sebelius*,[30] upholding the Affordable Care Act, known to most Americans as "Obamacare." The Constitution was designed to protect individual liberty by enclosing the federal government inside a fence of enumerated powers. *Raich* and *Sebelius* show what happens when the rails of that fence are replaced with rubber bands.

Angel Raich suffers from a number of severe medical conditions, including fibromyalgia, seizures, and an inoperable brain tumor.[31] Because she is allergic to most synthetic drugs, medical cannabis provides her sole relief from the excruciating pain of her various conditions. It also helps her sleep, relieves nausea, and prevents muscle spasms. "Without cannabis," she says on her website, "my life would be a death sentence."[32] Unable to cultivate her own plants, Ms. Raich was assisted by two nearby "caregivers" who grew marijuana and supplied it to her free of charge.

Though medical cannabis is legal in Raich's home state of California, federal law flatly prohibits the use of marijuana, even under a doctor's care in states that have authorized it. After federal agents raided the home of another medical cannabis user, Diane Monson, and seized six plants she was growing at home for her own use, Raich and Monson filed suit challenging the constitutionality of the federal Controlled Substances Act as applied to their particular circumstances. Their argument was straightforward: unlike states, Congress has no general authority to enact criminal laws and must therefore point to some specific grant of power in the Constitution. The federal government responded, predictably, by invoking its power to regulate interstate commerce. Just one small problem: the marijuana at issue in *Raich* was grown in California, was given (not sold) to Raich and Monson, and never left the state. So the question was: does Congress's power to regulate "commerce" "among" the states enable it to criminalize the purely local, entirely noncommercial distribution of a homegrown plant?

Absolutely, said the Supreme Court. Writing for a 6-3 majority, Justice Stevens explained that if Congress wants to criminalize purely local, noncommercial activities—like growing a plant in your back yard and giving it to a neighbor—all it has to do is assert the general power to regulate the "national market" in that item by creating what he euphemistically called a "closed regulatory system," meaning a national ban.[33] Under the aggregation principle embraced by the Court in *Wickard*, any transaction or exchange, no matter how trivial, may be characterized as potentially frustrating Congress's plan for total control of any given activity.

In the seventy years between *Wickard v. Filburn* in 1942 and the Obamacare decision in 2012, the Supreme Court found only two things to lie beyond Congress's constitutionally enumerated powers: making it illegal to possess a gun within a thousand feet of a school, and allowing victims of gender-motivated violence to sue their attackers in federal court.[34] In both of these cases, however, the scope of the law was quite narrow and did not seriously threaten the balance of power between state and federal governments.

So the question remained whether the Supreme Court would go to bat for federalism when it really mattered—in the face of a law that represented the kind of massive federal power-grab that the Constitution was specifically designed to prevent. The answer came in *NFIB v. Sebelius*, the challenge to the constitutionality of Obamacare, which is perhaps the most sweeping assertion of federal power since the New Deal. At the heart of Obamacare lay an unprecedented requirement that all Americans purchase government-approved health insurance or pay a penalty for failing to do so. Challengers argued that none of the usual ploys for exercising unenumerated federal powers would work in this case, particularly since Congress was not seeking to regulate existing economic activity but rather to force people to engage in economic activity against their will and then regulate it.

The good news is that five justices rejected the federal government's Orwellian claim that the constitutional power to regulate commerce among the states includes the authority to regulate individuals who have chosen not to participate in commerce. As Chief Justice Roberts explained, "the government's logic would justify a mandatory purchase to solve almost any problem."[35] For example, many Americans do not eat a healthy diet, and their failure to do so increases health-care costs "to a greater extent than the failure of the uninsured to purchase insurance."[36] On the government's reading of the commerce clause, Congress could address this problem by forcing everyone to buy vegetables.[37] Moreover, besides food and health care, the list of things most people will need at some point in their lives goes on and on—including clothing, shelter, education, transportation, and entertainment—and people all over the country choose not to participate in one or more of those markets every single day. The Supreme Court came one vote from accepting the proposition that Congress is empowered to regulate individual decisions about whether and how to participate in every one of those industries. For example, you may have spent all day today, as many other people did, not buying an electric car. You might think that was your prerogative; it appears four justices on the Supreme Court do not.

But five justices refused to buy the commerce clause argument. With Old Reliable off the table, the feds had to get creative. As usual, they rose to the challenge. In a striking about-face, administration lawyers argued that the requirement to purchase health insurance was not really a "requirement" after all, but simply a private choice with varying tax consequences. Thus, contrary to the actual text of the law, Americans would not be "penalized" for failing to obtain government-approved health insurance. Instead, they would simply have to pay somewhat more in taxes for deciding to forgo it.

In making that argument, the government's lawyers were directly contradicting President Obama, who repeatedly denied that the health-care law imposed any new taxes, as did its supporters in Congress.[38] Bolstering this point, the Affordable Care Act itself refers to the payment required from people who forgo health insurance as a "penalty" some eighteen times, and even the chief justice recognized that "[t]he most straightforward reading of the mandate is that it *commands* individuals to purchase insurance."[39] To avoid declaring Obamacare unconstitutional, however, the Supreme Court looked at it not from the standpoint of what Congress *actually* did—enact a law that requires people to buy health insurance and imposes a financial penalty for failing to do so—but rather what Congress *could* have done, which is impose higher taxes on people who choose not to obtain government-approved health insurance.

According to Chief Justice Roberts, the Court's duty was not to base its ruling on the "most natural interpretation" of the law, but instead on any "fairly possible" reading of the law that would result in its being upheld. Thus, "every reasonable construction must be resorted to, in order to save the statute from unconstitutionality," even to the point of asserting, by implication, that the president and members of Congress either misled the American people when they insisted the individual mandate was not a tax or simply had no idea what they were talking about.[40] But as Judge Roger Vinson had commented in his decision striking down the law earlier in district court,

Congress should not be permitted to secure and cast politically difficult votes on controversial legislation by deliberately calling something one thing, after which the defenders of that legislation take an "Alice-in-Wonderland" tack and argue in court that Congress really meant something else entirely, thereby circumventing the safeguard that exists to keep their broad power in check.[41]

Among the supposed virtues of judicial restraint is respect for the results of the political process. But when deference becomes collaboration, as in the Obamacare decision, it undermines political accountability and distorts the system of checks and balances upon which our freedom depends.

DEATH BY DEFERENCE

Much of modern constitutional law involves figuring out how to take difficult cases and make them easy by removing any significant element of judgment. In effect, what courts do is substitute labels for principles and then decide cases based on whatever label seems to apply. And while it certainly makes life easier for judges, the result is that government gets to do some pretty awful things to people without much of a reason.

Consider the framework that judges use to decide cases involving constitutional rights that are neither specifically listed in the text of the Constitution nor among the handful of unenumerated rights—like interstate travel or raising one's own children[42]—that the Supreme Court has chosen to recognize so far. It's a heads-the-government-wins/tails-the-citizen-loses test that Randy Barnett calls the "*Glucksberg* two-step."[43]

Washington v. Glucksberg[44] was a 1997 case in which the Supreme Court upheld a Washington state law prohibiting assisted suicide. The plaintiffs in that case—several terminally ill patients, their doctors, and a nonprofit—argued that there is a constitutional right to take one's own life and to have the assistance of others if need be. The Supreme Court rejected that claim, and while the decision is certainly defensible from a legal standpoint, the Court's reasoning created a deadly trap for people trying to vindicate rights not specifically enumerated in the Constitution.

Here's how the trap works: In order to be treated as "fundamental" and thus eligible for meaningful judicial protection, a right not specifically enumerated in the Constitution must be given a "careful description" by the person asserting it and must appear to be a freedom that is "deeply rooted in this Nation's history and tradition."[45] While it may not have been the Supreme Court's intent, this framework has become the judicial version of a rigged carnival game: frame the proposed right broadly enough to meet the "deeply rooted in this Nation's history" requirement and you will flunk the "careful description" requirement; frame the proposed right narrowly enough to meet the "careful description" requirement and you will flunk the "deeply rooted" requirement. That may sound terribly abstract, but the stakes for real people can be enormous.

Consider the plight of gravely ill people for whom no FDA-approved treatment has worked. Their last remaining option may well be to try experimental therapies, knowing full well that those treatments may not work and could even hasten their deaths. Might that be a rational decision for people in that position to make? Absolutely. Do they have a constitutional right to make that decision? That was the question posed in *Abigail Alliance for Better Access to Developmental Drugs v. Eschenbach*.[46]

In 2003, a group of terminally ill cancer patients filed suit against the FDA seeking access to experimental drugs that might save their lives. Incredibly, the FDA had blocked access to those drugs on the grounds that they might be too dangerous for the patients—again, that's terminally ill cancer patients—to take. Even more incredibly, a federal appellate court agreed. Here's what happened.

As framed by the plaintiffs seeking to provide a sufficiently "careful" description to survive the first part of the *Glucksberg* two-step, the question was whether the Constitution protects "the right of a terminally ill patient with no remaining approved treatment options" to have access to "investigational medications" that have passed Phase I clinical testing, meaning they have been found safe enough for significant human testing.[47] In refusing to acknowledge that right as fundamental, the majority made no serious effort to weigh the actual interests at stake on either side of the case: the ability of terminally ill people to take desperate measures to save their own lives, on the one hand, versus the government's stated desire to protect people from the hazards of unapproved drugs on the other. Instead, the majority simply examined the historical record and concluded that the right to take experimental drugs in an effort to save one's own life is not "deeply rooted in our Nation's history and traditions." Accordingly, the majority treated the right as nonfundamental, applied rational basis review, and rubber-stamped the FDA's decision to prevent terminally ill people from taking potentially life-saving drugs.

Two judges on the D.C. Circuit Court of Appeals, Judith Ann Rogers and Douglas Ginsburg, rejected the majority's judge-by-labels approach and gave serious consideration to whether access to potentially life-saving medical care should be considered a significant constitutional right. As the dissenting judges noted, the majority opinion "reflects a flawed conception of the right claimed" by the terminally ill patients "and a stunning misunderstanding of the stakes" for them.[48] The dissent went right to the heart of the dilemma created by the *Glucksberg* two-step: "As the [majority's] opinion in this case demonstrates, the description of the right is of crucial importance—too broad and a right becomes all-encompassing and impossible to evaluate; too narrow and a right appears trivial."[49] Properly conceived, the right at issue in *Abigail Alliance* was the right "to attempt to preserve one's life." The dissent warned that "[t]o deny the constitutional importance of the right to life and to attempt to preserve life is to move from judicial modesty to judicial abdication, as well as confusion."[50] Unfortunately, the Supreme Court refused to hear the case, and the majority decision stands.

In reducing to practical nullities the contract clause, the Fifth Amendment's protection against eminent domain for private use, the doctrine of enumerated federal powers, and the Ninth Amendment's recognition of unenumerated rights, the Supreme Court's behavior has been neither sporadic nor accidental. And lower courts have followed suit, protecting government prerogatives at the expense of liberty.

Unfortunately, these are merely symptoms of a deeper dysfunction, a conviction that judges should defer to members of the other branches regarding the constitutional limits of their own power and that courts should enforce such limits only "with reluctance."[51] Though seriously misguided, that impulse isn't new. In fact, following the Civil War it led a bare majority of the Supreme Court to neuter the Fourteenth Amendment and render its protections for liberty a dead letter just when they were needed most. It is to that tragic episode that we turn now.

CHAPTER 5

Liberty Slaughtered

The Founders were brilliant but not perfect. One of their biggest mistakes was believing that state governments, being close to the people, presented little threat to individual liberty. But they were dead wrong about that, as many Americans quickly discovered. The Fourteenth Amendment was added to the Constitution in 1868 in order to correct the Founders' mistake and empower the federal government to protect people from the tyranny of state and local officials. But five Supreme Court justices thought that was a bad idea and effectively nullified the Fourteenth Amendment by ripping out its heart, the privileges or immunities clause, in an 1873 decision aptly named the *Slaughter-House Cases*.

The Court has tried to mitigate that error in various ways over the past century, but these efforts have been ad hoc and unpersuasive. Presented with a golden opportunity just three years ago to correct its misunderstanding of the privileges or immunities clause, the Court whiffed. With the exception of Clarence Thomas, the justices are evidently not interested in revisiting a constitutional provision that should have been, and still could be, an important source of liberty in the Constitution.

The Fourteenth Amendment was designed to correct an error occasioned by a travesty. The travesty was slavery, the status of which was not resolved or even addressed by the original Constitution. The error was having the Bill of Rights apply only to the federal government and not the states. This appears to have been a deliberate choice on the part of the Framers, motivated in part by a desire to omit anything from the Constitution that might appear to threaten the institution of slavery. Besides challenging the legality of slavery itself, making the Bill of Rights applicable against the states would have raised doubts about the often draconian measures that Southern states used to protect the system, including the ruthless suppression of abolitionist sentiment.[1]

Though leading abolitionists and others argued that the Constitution obligated states to respect individual rights, the Supreme Court unambiguously rejected that position in *Barron v. Baltimore* (1833).[2] Consequently, state and local governments were free to censor speech, deny the right of assembly, and disregard other provisions in the Bill of Rights, which many of them did. These abuses became more acute in the aftermath of the Civil War, when Southern states tried to keep blacks in a condition of constructive servitude through the continued violation of basic civil rights including particularly the freedom to speak, work, travel, own property, and enter into contracts. Oppressing newly freed blacks and their white supporters required states to suppress one more right as well, which they did systematically and with great determination: the right to own guns for self-defense.

The history is shocking and undisputed. Discharged Union soldiers, white and black, were forcibly stripped of their weapons by officials throughout the South. It was reported that in one Kentucky town, "the town marshal takes all arms from returned colored soldiers and is very prompt in shooting the blacks whenever an opportunity occurs," while outlaws "make brutal attacks and raids upon freedmen, who are defenseless, for the civil law-officers disarm the colored man and hand him over to armed marauders."[3] And it wasn't just guns. South Carolina law prescribed flogging for any black man who broke a labor contract, while laws in other states prohibited blacks from practicing trades or even leaving their employer's land without permission. Children of former slaves in Mississippi were "taken from their parents and bound out to the planters," while Union sympathizers often had their property seized or found themselves banished from a state outright.[4]

These acts were widely reported, stirring up public outrage and prompting calls for action. Congress moved swiftly to curb the abuses, both through legislation and, when doubts were raised as to the constitutionality of these laws, by amending the Constitution. For instance, the Civil Rights Act of 1866 established birthright citizenship for all Americans regardless of race and provided that all citizens must have the same right to make and enforce contracts, appear in court, own property, and enjoy "the equal benefit of all laws and proceedings . . . as is enjoyed by white citizens."[5] Any doubts about the constitutionality of this law were resolved by the Fourteenth Amendment, which was designed to empower the federal government to stamp out a culture of lawless oppression in which newly free blacks and their white supporters were systematically silenced, terrorized, and abused.

Section 1 of the Fourteenth Amendment contains three substantive limits on the power of state governments: it provides that no state may deprive any person of life, liberty, or property without due process of law; no state may deny any person equal protection of the laws; and no state shall "make or enforce any law which shall abridge the privileges or immunities of citizens of the United States."[6] That last clause was meant to be the workhorse of the amendment. Unlike today, the term "privileges or immunities" was in common use at the time the Fourteenth Amendment was drafted and appears to have been synonymous with the word "rights" as we now understand it.[7]

Exactly which rights were included within the ambit of the "privileges or immunities of citizens of the United States" could not be fully enumerated in the Fourteenth Amendment, any more than they could be in the Bill of Rights.[8] It is not difficult to understand why: the oppression of freedmen and white Unionists, although partially reflected in the notorious Black Codes of the time, was not confined to any particular set of laws or some official policy that could be identified and proscribed. Instead, it was an ethos, a determination to maintain the vestiges of a slave culture in defiance of the nation's determination to end it. The idea that a constitutional provision designed to eliminate such a culture could be drafted with perfect and comprehensive clarity is untenable. Yet that is the basis upon which various scholars and judges have advocated ignoring the privileges or immunities clause, starting with the five-justice majority in the *Slaughter-House Cases*.[9]

Slaughter-House involved a constitutional challenge by a group of butchers to a Louisiana law that created a state-chartered monopoly on the sale and slaughter of animals in New Orleans. The law did not prevent the butchers from working, but it required them to do so in a slaughterhouse operated by a single company to which they were required to pay various fees in return for using its facility.[10] The butchers claimed that prohibiting them from working independently constituted a violation of their rights under the Thirteenth and Fourteenth Amendments, which had not yet been interpreted by the Supreme Court.[11] In particular, they argued that among the "privileges or immunities" protected by the Fourteenth Amendment was the right to earn a living in the occupation of their choice free from unreasonable and, more specifically, anticompetitive government regulations.[12]

In dismissing the butchers' claims, the majority began by rejecting the factual premise on which they were based. According to Justice Samuel F. Miller, "a critical examination of the act hardly justifies [the butchers'] assertions" that it deprived them of the ability to practice their trade.[13] The majority went on to assert that the due process, equal protection, and privileges or immunities clauses of the Fourteenth Amendment were not intended to significantly alter the balance of power between the federal and state governments. According to Justice Miller, the privileges or immunities clause secured only a narrow and rather trivial set of rights of national citizenship, such as access to navigable waterways and the ability to invoke the protection of the federal government when on the high seas.[14] But those were not the rights over which we fought a civil war, nor were they the rights whose systematic violation prompted the adoption of the Fourteenth Amendment.

Justice Miller's opinion in *Slaughter-House* is sloppy and unpersuasive. He is plainly reasoning backward from a preferred result, which is the nullification of an amendment designed to provide federal protection of individual rights against state and local officials. In support of that result, Justice Miller misquotes constitutional text,[15] ignores both history and contemporaneous events, and defies popular understanding—all because of his personal conviction that giving the privileges or immunities clause its intended effect would "radically" shift power from the states to the federal government.[16]

The majority's reasoning was systematically demolished in three dissenting opinions. As Justice Stephen Field correctly observed, the majority's construction of the Fourteenth Amendment, particularly the privileges or immunities clause, rendered it "a vain and idle enactment, which accomplished nothing."[17] Similarly, after conducting a more searching (and forthright) analysis of the relevant text and history than did the majority, Justice Joseph P. Bradley concluded that "it was the intention of the people of this country in adopting [the Fourteenth Amendment] to provide National security against violation by the States of the fundamental rights of the citizen."[18] Justice Noah Haynes Swayne, too, recognized the majority's defiance of popular will, observing that its construction of the Fourteenth Amendment "defeats, by a limitation not anticipated, the intent of those by whom the instrument was framed and of those by whom it was adopted."[19]

Few if any constitutional provisions have attracted more academic attention than the Fourteenth Amendment, including the privileges or immunities clause. Given the breadth and ideological diversity of this scholarship, it is striking that a strong consensus has emerged: simply put, virtually everyone now agrees that *Slaughter-House* misinterpreted the privileges or immunities clause.[20] The majority's conclusions, as the historian Eric Foner put it, "should have been seriously doubted by anyone who read the Congressional debates of the 1860s."[21] And Professor Thomas McAffee has observed that the Supreme Court's misinterpretation of that provision "is one of the few important constitutional issues about which virtually every modern commentator is in agreement."[22]

The Supreme Court's abdication in *Slaughter-House* produced a bitter harvest, including the advent of Jim Crow, a system of racial segregation and oppression that the Fourteenth Amendment was in part designed to prevent. Besides its human toll, Justice Miller's misinterpretation of the privileges or immunities clause fundamentally warped the Supreme Court's jurisprudence of rights in a manner that persists to this day. Having drained the Fourteenth Amendment of any real force early on, the Court left itself in the untenable position of either standing by while state and local officials continued to violate basic civil rights, or figuring out some way to sidestep its original mistake without actually correcting it.

The Court accomplished the latter by turning to the due process clause, which it used to "incorporate" most of the two dozen or so separate provisions in the Bill of Rights into the Fourteenth Amendment and make them applicable against state and local governments. The Supreme Court has also used the due process clause to protect a handful of unenumerated rights, including the freedom to travel, marry, and have children.

This approach to enforcing certain rights against the states has come to be called "substantive due process." And while it has a much stronger textual basis and historical pedigree than its opponents typically acknowledge, the idea that the due *process* clause might also refer to *substantive* rights strikes many as incongruous. Justice Scalia is among the most vocal critics of substantive due process, and he seldom misses an opportunity to disparage the concept. But as we recently learned, even Justice Scalia is willing to embrace substantive due process when the only alternatives are either to withhold protection from a right he believes in or to revive the privileges or immunities clause by overturning *Slaughter-House*. These tensions came to a head in the two gun-rights cases decided by the Supreme Court in 2008 and 2010.

After allowing the Second Amendment to lie dormant for more than two centuries, the Supreme Court held in *District of Columbia v. Heller* (2008) that it protects an individual right to own guns in federal jurisdictions like Washington D.C.[23] But because the Bill of Rights does not apply directly to the states, that left open the question whether the right to keep and bear arms would apply to state and local governments through the Fourteenth Amendment as well. The Supreme Court tackled this question two years later in a case called *McDonald v. City of Chicago*, where the Court got the answer right but not the reasoning.

McDonald involved a challenge to Chicago's restrictive gun laws brought by my *Heller* co-counsel, Alan Gura. Alan clerked at the Institute for Justice and shares IJ's belief that the Supreme Court misconstrued the privileges or immunities clause in the *Slaughter-House Cases*. He also agrees that the Court should correct that mistake instead of limping along with an ad hoc theory of substantive due process that some justices apparently do not even believe in. Accordingly, Alan did something in *McDonald* that very few lawyers would have done: he invited the Supreme Court to revisit *Slaughter-House* by protecting gun ownership from state infringement using the constitutional provision that was actually designed to do that job—the privileges or immunities clause of the Fourteenth Amendment.

Only Clarence Thomas accepted that invitation. In a lone concurrence, Justice Thomas explained in meticulous detail, with extensive citations to historical data largely absent from the plurality and dissenting opinions, why the right to own a gun for self-defense is most plausibly protected by the privileges or immunities clause.[24] None of the justices in the plurality or the dissent took serious issue with Justice Thomas's analysis or even bothered to engage it in any serious way. Instead, all of the other justices simply assumed that the privileges-or-immunities argument was foreclosed by the Court's intellectually indefensible holding in the *Slaughter-House Cases*.[25]

Justice Alito, joined by Roberts, Scalia, and Kennedy, wrote a conventional opinion in which he argued that the Second Amendment right to keep and bears arms is incorporated against the states through the due process clause of the Fourteenth Amendment. Although he acknowledged the weight of scholarly opinion against the Supreme Court's interpretation of the privileges or immunities clause in *Slaughter-House*, Justice Alito explained that they saw "no need to reconsider that interpretation here" because the Court had been using the due process clause to protect individual rights for "many decades."[26]

In fact, there are many reasons for revisiting *Slaughter-House*, starting with the fact that it is the first major Supreme Court decision interpreting what is arguably the most important amendment to the Constitution—and everyone knows it's wrong. Indeed, as Justice Alito notes in his *McDonald* opinion, virtually no serious modern scholar, "'left, right, or center,'" thinks *Slaughter-House* is a plausible reading of the Fourteenth Amendment, and there is an "overwhelming consensus" among leading constitutional scholars that the opinion is not only wrong but "'egregiously wrong.'"[27] It smacks of hubris to assume that the Supreme Court's misinterpretation of the privileges or immunities clause in *Slaughter-House* makes no difference today because the Court has managed to cobble together a slapdash theory of liberty from the remaining pieces of the Fourteenth Amendment.[28]

Justice Scalia underscores this point in his concurring opinion in *McDonald* when he explains that he joins the Court's decision to protect gun ownership under the Fourteenth Amendment despite his "misgivings" about the plurality's use of substantive due process to achieve that result.[29] Scalia says he has "acquiesced" in the Supreme Court's "incorporation of certain guarantees in the Bill of Rights" as a matter of longstanding precedent, but he is coy about whether he thinks that precedent is right or wrong.[30] His agnosticism about one of the most important questions in all of constitutional law—whether the Fourteenth Amendment protects individual rights from state infringement— is striking, and one might suppose that a self-professed textualist like Justice Scalia would strive to get it right based on a complete reading of the amendment. What he and many like-minded conservatives do instead is disparage the idea of protecting individual rights through substantive due process while refusing to consider whether the privileges or immunities clause, properly understood, does precisely that.[31]

If federal courts are going to be in the business of protecting individual rights from infringement by state and local governments, which is what the framers of the Fourteenth Amendment plainly intended, then they should do so on the basis of a coherent interpretation of the relevant text. The Supreme Court's continued failure to embrace that standard has resulted in a stunted and incomplete jurisprudence of liberty.

CHAPTER 6

Why Do Judges Abdicate?

To recap, we have a judiciary that refuses to enforce the concept of enumerated federal powers in any serious way; that has rendered functionally meaningless the contract clause, the privileges or immunities clause of the Fourteenth Amendment, and the Fifth Amendment's prohibition against taking property for private use; and that provides no meaningful protection for rights deemed "nonfundamental" by the Supreme Court. We have a judiciary that will ensure the government is pursuing a legitimate state interest in some settings but not others. We have a judiciary that requires the government to support its factual assertions with evidence in some constitutional cases but not others. And we have a judiciary that will sometimes rewrite statutes and invent justifications for laws in order to avoid saying no to government.

In short, I believe the *fact* that courts sometimes abdicate their duty to enforce constitutional limits on government power is beyond dispute. The question is why? I do not pretend to have an authoritative answer, but I have some solid hunches based on my experience litigating constitutional cases and reading countless judicial opinions in the twenty years I have been a lawyer. I think it largely boils down to a few basic points.

First, most judges would undoubtedly resist the idea that they are abdicating their duties, both because they get their marching orders from the Supreme Court and because they honestly see no serious problems with the current approach. Second is a fundamentally unrealistic perception of the way policy is made. Modern constitutional doctrine assumes that laws are generally enacted for public-spirited reasons after careful legislative deliberation; but there is strong evidence that often this is not the case. As a result, courts that apply a strong presumption of constitutionality to challenged laws are likely to err, especially when the presumption is essentially irrebuttable, as it tends to be in rational basis cases.[1] Third is a tendency to overemphasize majoritarianism at the expense of constitutionalism, for example, by striking down only those laws that are *unambiguously* prohibited. Whatever its populist appeal might be, that approach demands of the Constitution a level of specificity that it simply was not designed to provide. I referred to this earlier as the bullet-point Constitution.

I believe abdication is prompted by external factors as well, including often baseless charges of judicial activism that appear to have more to do with influencing how courts act than with honestly describing their performance. I take up that point in the next chapter. The remainder of this chapter will consider how adherence to erroneous government-favoring precedent, misperceptions about policymaking, and mistaken assumptions about majority rule all contribute to the systemic under-enforcement of constitutional limits on government power by the courts.

JUST FOLLOWING PRECEDENT

The intensity of the public backlash when the Supreme Court upheld the use of eminent domain in *Kelo v. City of New London* (2005) surprised many constitutional elites, including judges and law professors.[2] From their perspective, *Kelo* featured the routine application of longstanding precedent to produce a wholly unexceptional result. In a sense they were right: courts have been rubber-stamping the use of eminent domain for more than half a century, so the real surprise would have been if the property owners had won instead of the city. What the constitutional elites apparently failed to realize is that most people don't follow Supreme Court precedent. And it was news to most Americans—very unwelcome news—that the Supreme Court considers owning a home or small business a nonfundamental right unworthy of significant judicial protection. Simply put, if a politically connected property developer or big-box store has the wherewithal to convince a city council or redevelopment agency to grab your beachfront house or your family-owned brake shop on the corner of the busiest intersection in town, the Constitution has nothing to say about it as far as the Supreme Court is concerned.[3]

The point is that what passes for unremarkable precedent among judges, scholars, and practitioners of constitutional law may be quite surprising to ordinary Americans, and it may well be a mistake to assume that the longstanding existence of a particular practice— such as rubber-stamping the government's use of eminent domain to transfer property from one private owner to another—equates to public acceptance. Moreover, it can take a special case to impress upon people the full implications of a given practice that may have seemed less threatening in the abstract.

For example, the Supreme Court's most significant eminent domain decision immediately before *Kelo* was a 1984 case called *Hawaii Housing Authority v. Midkiff*.[4] *Midkiff* involved an attempt to break up concentrated land ownership on the island of Oahu through the forced sale of property from landlords to tenants. As usual in property-rights cases, the Supreme Court applied a highly deferential standard of review, but it did so in a context that would not have prompted the average person to say, "Hey, wait a minute—that could happen to me." *Kelo* was a much different case. In *Kelo*, the government wanted to bulldoze an entire working-class neighborhood and replace it with upscale housing and high-end commercial space. As most people realized, that *could* happen to just about anyone. Indeed, Justice O'Connor, who penned the *Midkiff* decision, made clear in her *Kelo* dissent that she appreciated the distinction when she asked rhetorically, "who among us can say she already makes the most productive or attractive possible use of her property?"[5] The intense reaction to *Kelo* shows that Americans got the point. While very few of us are at risk of having our homes taken in order to correct a land oligopoly or even build a privately owned railroad or hospital, virtually all of us are at risk of having our homes or businesses taken if the only question is whether a politically connected property developer can convince a cash-strapped state or local government that he might put the land to more profitable use.

Again, the fact that the Supreme Court is simply applying longstanding precedent in a given case does not mean that it is not abdicating. For those who strongly support constitutionally limited government, among the clearest examples of a case that represents both longstanding precedent and glaring abdication is *Wickard v. Filburn*—the case involving the Ohio farmer who was fined by the federal government for growing more than his allotted share of wheat.[6] Over the past seventy years, *Wickard* has been cited by the Supreme Court sixty-five times, and several hundred times in the federal appellate courts, yet it remains an intensely controversial decision, at least outside the halls of academia. And it is easy to see why. People understand that *Wickard* is very much like *Kelo* in that each signifies the elimination of any meaningful limits on government power in a particular area of law—federalism-based limits on Congress and the public-use requirement for eminent domain, respectively.

Judges on lower courts are of course bound to apply Supreme Court precedent in cases arising under the U.S. Constitution whether they agree with it or not. But lower-court judges often have significant discretion in deciding which precedents to apply, and the fact that the Supreme Court hears only sixty or seventy cases of the thousands presented to it each year means that the ruling of a federal appellate court or state supreme court will generally be the last word in any given case.

In the Florida interior design case mentioned earlier, for example, we raised a cutting-edge question of constitutional law regarding the intersection of free speech and occupational licensing that the Supreme Court has not yet answered. The question involves the status of so-called "speaking professions," meaning occupations in which the product or service provided consists entirely of speech. This includes lawyers, who write contracts and legal briefs, argue in court, and provide verbal or written advice to their clients, along with a host of other vocations—from teachers and therapists to business consultants—whose work consists of providing information and opinion rather than physical labor or manufactured goods.

The challenge for courts when confronted with laws affecting speaking professions lies in deciding which line of Supreme Court precedent to apply: free-speech cases, which typically involve rigorous scrutiny of government regulation, or economic liberty cases, which typically involve no meaningful scrutiny. Interior design is a paradigmatic speaking vocation in that it consists entirely of creating drawings, making suggestions, and offering advice about the use of space inside a building. But instead of grappling with what should have been a challenging constitutional question about whether the government should have to justify the censorship of interior-design-related speech by requiring a license to engage in it, the appellate court simply brushed the issue aside by characterizing "direct, personalized speech with clients" as "occupational conduct" to which the First Amendment does not apply.[7] The implications of that holding are staggering. Consistently applied, it would mean no constitutional protection for myriad occupations involving "direct, personalized speech with clients," such as political and business consultants, salesmen, teachers, coaches, and IT providers. The idea that government may censor speech simply by slapping a licensing requirement on those who engage in it is repugnant to the First Amendment. But because the Supreme Court has not yet said so explicitly, lower courts continue to have the last word on who may speak for a living and who may not. As demonstrated by the Florida interior design decision, which devoted less than a page to the entire First Amendment analysis, they can be remarkably cavalier about it.

It should be noted that some lower-court judges have pushed back against the Supreme Court's persistently government-favoring precedent, even while acknowledging that they are bound to apply it. A recent example involved the federal government's complex scheme for regulating the sale of milk. The law at issue, passed in 2006, targeted a particular dairy operation run by the Hettinga family in Arizona, who had been taking advantage of a loophole that enabled them to sell their milk directly to customers instead of participating in the collectivist scheme envisioned—but imperfectly implemented—by the federal government. Defending the law in court, the government claimed it was designed to address "disorderly marketing conditions," namely, the Hettingas' ability to undercut other dairies on price by operating outside the communal milk-marketing system.[8] In a terse, unsigned opinion, a three-judge panel of the D.C. Circuit Court of Appeals accepted that argument and dismissed the Hettingas' constitutional challenge. But even though they believed it was compelled by Supreme Court precedent, that result did not sit well with two members of the panel, as explained in a concurring opinion written by Judge Janice Rogers Brown and joined by Chief Judge David Sentelle.

Judge Brown begins by explaining that she agrees with the decision to dismiss the Hettingas' case because, based on her reading of longstanding precedents, "no other result is possible."[9] But after accepting her obligation to apply those precedents, she subjects them to a withering critique in which she argues that the Supreme Court has "abdicated its constitutional duty to protect economic rights."[10] The essence of that abdication, she says, is the judiciary's refusal to inquire whether the legislature's purpose and the means proposed to

advance it are truly "'within [the] legislative power.'"[11] After describing
the baleful influence of interest groups on the political process, Judge
Brown offers a stark assessment of the means by which the federal
government forced the Hettingas out of the free market and into
the collective milk-marketing scheme: "Neither the legislators nor
the lobbyists broke any positive laws to accomplish this result. It just
seems like a crime."[12] Her critique of the jurisprudence that compels
judges to stand by and do nothing in the face of such blatant government misconduct captures the essence of the problem this book
seeks to correct:

> The judiciary justifies its reluctance to intervene by claiming
> incompetence—apparently, judges lack the acumen to recog-
> nize corruption, self-interest, or arbitrariness in the economic
> realm—or deferring to the majoritarian imperative. The prac-
> tical effect of rational basis review of economic regulation is
> the absence of any check on the group interests that all too
> often control the democratic process. . . .
> Rational basis review means property is at the mercy of
> the pillagers.[13]

Judge Brown's strongly worded concurrence in *Hettinga v. United
States* was criticized by people who considered it intemperate or inde-
corous. Notably, they mostly took issue with the tone of her remarks,
not the substance. For it is difficult even for defenders of the status
quo to deny the substance of her critique of current case law. And
while the remaining judge on the panel declined to join the opinion,
he explained that he was "by no means unsympathetic to their criticism."[14] Courts rarely offer such a candid assessment because much of
modern constitutional law depends on denying—or at least ignoring—
the realities of the political process that Judge Brown confronted so
unsparingly in her opinion. But in fact there is an entire field of study
devoted to those realities, called public choice theory.

POLITICS WITHOUT ROMANCE

Public choice theory is, in the words of one of its founders, the study of "politics without romance."[15] It seeks to explain the workings of government and what actually motivates those who govern. Legislators tend to focus on increasing their likelihood of reelection, while bureaucrats normally seek to enlarge the budget, scope, and influence of the regulatory agency they work for. Public choice theory is relevant to the question of judicial engagement because it provides useful information about how confident or skeptical judges should be about the chances that any given policy was adopted for genuinely public-spirited reasons. If that happens most of the time and there is little reason to question the benevolent intentions of policymakers, then it makes sense for judges to show substantial deference to the political branches. But if this turns out to be incorrect—if it turns out that political decisions are frequently influenced by concerns other than promoting the general welfare—then it calls for greater vigilance, at least from a judiciary that is committed to fulfilling its role as a constitutional check on the other branches of government.

Lawmaking has been compared to making sausages. Modern constitutional doctrine calls for judges to act as if most of those sausages were being made in a sparkling clean laboratory by skilled technicians wearing latex gloves and hairnets. Public choice theory suggests otherwise. Indeed, the owner of a sausage factory near Washington D.C. remarked that he feels "insulted" when people compare his business to lawmaking.[16]

In ceding virtually all responsibility for ensuring constitutional compliance to the other branches in such areas as property rights, tax policy, business regulation, health care, and federalism, the judiciary makes a number of fundamental mistakes according to public choice theory. I will focus on two: the idea that the products of the political process reliably reflect majority will, and the belief that oppressive and unjust laws will eventually be repealed. Public choice theory makes clear that both of these assumptions are factually false. Here's why.

Getting a law enacted (or repealed) requires considerable effort. The sheer number of hurdles that must be overcome in order to do so strongly favors the status quo. And because people are busy with their own lives, they are likely to have neither the time nor the inclination to take a strong position on any given piece of legislation. Indeed, the vast majority of legislation has so little impact on any given individual that it is perfectly understandable if she takes no position on some particular legislation and makes no effort to learn anything about it either.[17] This opens the door for interest groups to exert tremendous influence over the political process by focusing on a small set of issues that their members care deeply about. The result, if those groups are effective at manipulating the process, will be policies that benefit their members but not necessarily the public at large. Agricultural subsidies are a familiar example. Following World War II, the federal government began subsidizing the production of wool in order to ensure a steady supply for military uniforms. The military switched to synthetic fibers and removed wool from its list of strategic materials in 1960. As a result, the need for combat-ready domestically produced sheep textiles ended; the wool subsidy did not.

Besides subsidies, another way that interest groups exploit the political process is by using it to suppress competition. Recall Emerson's famous observation that if a man can make a better mousetrap then the world will beat a path to his door. But what about existing mousetrap companies whose inferior products are no longer selling; what will they do? They have two choices if they don't want to go out of business: either come up with a better, cheaper mousetrap, or use politics to hamstring the new guy. Research and development is expensive, time-consuming, and uncertain. You might well get a better return by hiring a lobbyist to promote a new law prohibiting the sale of new mousetrap designs until they have been approved by the Mousetrap Oversight Board (MOB).

This is no caricature. Public choice theory, which is almost universally accepted and has produced three Nobel Prizes, confirms that interest groups work hard to manipulate the political process for their own benefit. The ability to raise prices above what would be charged in an open market—one where anyone could sell new mousetraps without prior approval from the MOB—is referred to as an "economic rent," and the process by which above-market prices are extracted from consumers and transferred to politically influential industry groups is called "rent-seeking."[18] Public choice economics has shown that rent-seeking is pervasive and laws are routinely enacted for the sole benefit of interest groups at public expense. "Forcing competition to be overregulated is an age-old method of getting a leg up in business," writes the notorious felon-lobbyist Jack Abramoff in his book, *Capitol Punishment.*[19]

The power of small groups with strong common interests to manipulate the political process "frequently leads to a tyranny of the minority."[20] Thus, recipients of wasteful subsidies and beneficiaries of anticompetitive business regulations receive substantial benefits that the rest of us pay for in the form of higher taxes, above-market prices for goods and services, and a reduction in consumer choice. This dynamic of concentrated benefits and dispersed costs means the general public has little incentive to oppose any particular bit of special-interest legislation, and very little incentive to work for its repeal once it has been enacted.

This leads to the second major fallacy underlying the call for reflexive judicial restraint: namely, the assumption that bad laws will eventually be repealed. This represents the triumph of hope over experience. Judges should know better, and perhaps some of them do. But the idea that the political process in America is reliably self-correcting nevertheless remains deeply ingrained in the Supreme Court's approach to constitutional law. In upholding the Oklahoma law that effectively legislated opticians out of business in *Williamson v. Lee Optical*, Justice Douglas explained, "The day is gone when this Court uses the Due Process Clause of the Fourteenth Amendment to strike down [economic regulations] . . . because they may be unwise, improvident, or out of harmony with a particular school of thought. . . . For protection against abuses by legislatures the people must resort to the polls, not to the courts."[21]

What an extraordinary statement: for protection against "abuses"— not mistakes, misjudgments, or disagreements, but *abuses*—people must seek redress with the body that perpetrated those abuses in the first place. The idea that the political process provides a viable means of eliminating unjust laws and undoing the handiwork of special-interest groups is a central tenet of the call for judicial deference.[22] But as Judge Brown argued in her *Hettinga* concurrence, "[t]he hope of correction at the ballot box is purely illusory."[23] The same public choice literature that shows how common it is for interest groups to enact self-serving legislation also shows that if anything it is more difficult to get rid of such legislation once enacted than to prevent it from being enacted in the first place.

Charles Brown of Hagerstown, Maryland, knows this better than most people. Charles, his wife Pat, and their son Eric own Rest Haven Cemetery in the lovely rolling hills of western Maryland. Charles and Pat bought the cemetery in 1988, hoping to replace the funeral home that had burned down there a few years before. The community strongly supported their plan, and the Browns built a new funeral home on the property. But in Maryland, only state-licensed funeral directors are allowed to own funeral homes, so the state funeral board refused to let them open it.

Charles knew there was no good reason for that law. In forty-eight other states, funeral homes may be owned by any person or corporation, as long as a licensed funeral director oversees the day-to-day operations. Saying that only licensed funeral directors may own funeral homes is like saying only a licensed pilot may own an airline. It makes no sense from a policy standpoint, but perfect sense from the standpoint of industry insiders seeking to exclude outsiders. Do you suppose mom-and-pop hamburger joints would favor a law that prohibits national chains such as McDonald's or Burger King from owning restaurants in their state while simultaneously sandbagging local entrepreneurs with innovative business models, like the combination funeral home and cemetery that Charles Brown wanted to open? You bet they would, and in Maryland that's precisely what state-licensed morticians managed to pull off in the funeral industry.

So Charles started knocking on doors at the state capitol in Annapolis. At first he was encouraged. Most of the legislators supported his proposal to repeal the restrictions on who may own a funeral home in Maryland, and not one of them believed the law was truly meant to help the public, as its proponents claimed. There were even letters from the Federal Trade Commission and the state health department confirming that restricting funeral-home ownership hurts consumers by discouraging competition, driving up prices, and limiting consumer choice. Charles worked tirelessly for ten years to get the law changed. He enlisted like-minded entrepreneurs, cemetery owners, and a fiery state delegate named Joanne Benson who knew from firsthand experience how unfair the law was. But no matter how much support they garnered, and no matter how feeble the arguments on the other side, they could never even get a repeal bill out of committee.

According to a front-page article in the *Washington Post*, the immovable legislative obstacle had a name: Hattie Harrison, a long-serving delegate with close ties to the Maryland funeral industry. Relating a conversation she had with a leading member of the industry who opposed repealing the ownership restrictions, Delegate Harrison said, "'He explained the whole thing to me. . . . He said they needed to keep things as they were in order to keep the big folk out.'"[24] So there you have it: naked economic protectionism for state-licensed funeral directors—and not just against the "big folk" from other states, but would-be innovators like Charles Brown as well.

As public choice theory and real-world experience both predict, the decade-long attempt to repeal Maryland's funeral-home law legislatively was unsuccessful. Unfortunately, so was Charles Brown's effort to challenge the law in court. In rejecting that challenge, a federal court of appeals admonished Mr. Brown, apparently without ironic intent, that "'[f]or protection against *abuses* by legislatures the people must resort to the polls, not to the courts.'"[25] But that is false. The Constitution was designed to protect people from legislative "abuses" like the use of government power to suppress competition and funnel monopoly profits to industry insiders. That courts allow those abuses to occur doesn't mean they are constitutional—it just ensures they will continue unabated as interest-group politics destroy the engine of American prosperity.

To be clear, it is not impossible to repeal rent-seeking laws like Maryland's restrictions on funeral-home ownership or Florida's interior design licensing law. It is also not impossible to win the lottery. But just as responsible people do not make winning the lottery a cornerstone of their financial planning, neither should the remote possibility of legislative repeal be a central tenet of judicial review.

MAJORITARIANISM VERSUS CONSTITUTIONALISM

I mentioned in the Introduction that one of the key misconceptions driving judicial abdication is the belief that ours is an essentially majoritarian political system. According to this view, the Constitution imposes a relatively small number of restrictions on government while leaving the rest up to the electoral process. As Judge Robert Bork put it in his influential book *The Tempting of America,* "in wide areas of life majorities are entitled to rule, if they wish, simply because they are majorities."[26] That is the distilled essence of what I call majoritarianism, and my sense is that most judges subscribe to some version of it. But they shouldn't, because democratic rule confers no special moral status on the policies adopted by majorities. Consider the following scenarios.

Imagine that your neighbor is keeping you awake by playing loud music late at night. You have two choices: you can try to persuade your neighbor to turn down the music, or you can call the police. If you went the first route, you'd have some pretty persuasive arguments. Playing loud music is inconsiderate, especially at night while most people are trying to sleep. You've noticed that your neighbor likes to sleep late on weekends, so how would he feel about you running your chainsaw outside his window at six in the morning? Also, there are young children in the neighborhood. Is it fair to keep them awake all night or else force their parents to soundproof their homes? Those are good arguments, and while not everyone would turn the music down in response, a reasonable person certainly would. In other words, you have a strong moral basis for asking—and expecting—your neighbor to turn down his music because he is using his property in a way that interferes with other people's ability to enjoy their own.

Now imagine that instead of playing loud music, your neighbor throws dinner parties at which he sometimes charges people for the cost of the food and his time spent preparing it. The parties are small, private affairs, and the only reason you know they're happening at all is because your neighbor told you about them. (This is not a hypothetical, by the way; do an Internet search for "underground supper clubs" and you'll see they are springing up in urban areas all over the country.) If you wanted your neighbor to stop throwing those dinner parties, would you have a compelling argument for why he should do so? An argument so strong that it would be unreasonable for your neighbor not to change his behavior, like the midnight rocker? The answer is no: your neighbor's private supper club is really none of your business. In fact, *you're* the one who's being unreasonable. Assuming the guests are not creating a traffic problem or coming and going at all hours, you are left with nothing more than an arbitrary disapproval of your neighbor's supper club (perhaps because you've not been invited).

But imagine you find another neighbor who also objects to the parties, and the two of you vote for an ordinance prohibiting them. The neighbor who hosts the supper clubs votes against the ordinance, but his is the only other vote cast, so the ordinance is adopted. Supper clubs are now illegal in your cul-de-sac.

The key difference between majoritarianism and constitutionalism is that with majoritarianism you don't have to give any reason for banning supper clubs—you just need the votes. But with constitutionalism, you need the votes *and* a legitimate reason. What is a legitimate reason? As discussed in Chapter 1, it must be something that is within the police power of the state, like preventing epidemics or fraudulent business practices. By contrast, things like spite or envy—or, as H. L. Mencken said of Puritans, the "haunting fear that someone, somewhere, may be happy"—do not provide a legitimate basis for interfering with another person's freedom, no matter how many people vote for it.

Majoritarians disagree. They reject the idea that the Constitution requires government to pursue only public-spirited ends; instead, they regard the democratic process as, in effect, self-legitimizing. You like to eat French fries; I'm afraid you'll get fat. You want to grow vegetables in your front yard; I think they look ugly. You want to have children; I don't think you should. An intellectually consistent majoritarian would say that because the Constitution does not specifically address any of those things, if I can get enough people to vote for laws prohibiting you from eating French fries, or growing vegetables in your yard, or having children, then that's the end of it. We owe you no explanation, and our reasons for enacting those laws—good, bad, or arbitrary—are "entirely irrelevant."[27]

But the Supreme Court has never fully embraced the majoritarian ethic, and for good reason. Contrary to Judge Bork's glib assertion, there is no moral, philosophical, or constitutional basis for the proposition that political majorities are "entitled" to rule simply because they are majorities. Nor is there a strong practical argument for it either. Throughout history, including the history of this country, political majorities have embraced profoundly immoral policies, from slavery and eugenics to the racial apartheid of Jim Crow. Accordingly, even in those "wide areas of life" not specifically addressed by the Constitution—which include everything from getting married and having a family to putting food on your table and how to spend your free time—the Supreme Court nevertheless requires that there be a rational relationship between the regulation and a *legitimate* governmental purpose.[28]

The problem, as discussed in Chapter 3, is how much wiggle room the courts find in the word "rational." So much, it turns out, that the constitutionality of a given law often depends on the government's willingness to misrepresent its true ends in court. Compare these two scenarios involving a constitutional challenge to a (nonhypothetical)[29] law requiring a private investigator's license to repair computers:

Scenario 1—Candid Government Lawyer

Judge: Counsel, does this law serve a legitimate governmental purpose?

CGL: Not as far as I can tell, your honor. There have been no consumer complaints, no problems with incompetent practitioners, and no reported incidents where anyone's computer has been broken, stolen, or otherwise mishandled while being repaired. Moreover, there is no requirement that private investigators know anything about computer repair or have any particular competence in that area. I honestly can't see any way this law could benefit the public.

Judge: Where did it come from then?

CGL: From the private investigators' trade association, your honor. They drafted it, they lobbied for it, and they got the legislature to pass it verbatim.

Judge: So this law was enacted to benefit private investigators by giving them a monopoly on computer repair?

CGL: Truthfully, yes. Without the slightest doubt.

Scenario 2—Savvy Government Lawyer

Judge: Counsel, does this law serve a legitimate governmental purpose?

SGL: Respectfully, your honor, that is not the relevant question in cases involving nonfundamental rights like occupational freedom. The relevant question is whether we can *imagine* that this law might serve a legitimate governmental purpose—not whether it actually does.

Judge: So the government contends this law is rationally related to a *conceivable* public purpose?

SGL: Absolutely, your honor. This law *could* have been passed to protect the public from incompetent or unethical practitioners. It *could* have been passed to ensure that if a customer has a bad experience there's a specific licensing board they can complain to.

Judge: Is that a truthful answer, counsel?

SGL: It's . . . a legally sufficient answer, your honor.

I realize, of course, that things are not always so clear-cut. But sometimes they are. For instance, Louisiana's florist licensing law was plainly enacted for the purpose of shielding state-licensed florists from fair competition. It has no more to do with protecting the public from incompetent practitioners than it does with ensuring the security of America's nuclear arsenal. I think it is wrong to permit the government to misrepresent its true ends in court and wrong to reward it for doing so by upholding laws that have no *genuine* public purpose. But majoritarians do not require the government to give an honest explanation for restricting people's freedom; in fact, they don't require any explanation at all. That is the very essence of arbitrary government, and it is precisely what the Founders fought to get rid of—not create.

THE BULLET-POINT CONSTITUTION

Another driver of abdication is judges who demand greater specificity from the Constitution than it was designed to provide. Constitutions are not meant to be bullet-point lists. They do not explain in minute detail every little thing government may and may not do. Instead, constitutions are designed to establish a machinery of government—the process for electing representatives and enacting laws, the allocation of responsibilities among different branches, etc.—and to provide guidelines for how government power may be exercised. Sometimes those guidelines are quite specific, as when the U.S. Constitution establishes a minimum age for senators, representatives, and the president; but often they are more general, such as granting Congress the authority to regulate commerce among the states and to "make all Laws which shall be necessary and proper for carrying into Execution" the powers delegated to the federal government by the Constitution.

While most judges surely understand in theory that the Constitution was not designed to provide a specific answer to every question that might arise concerning the interaction between individuals and government, they often saddle it with that requirement in practice. The result is a tendency to hold that anything not specifically forbidden to the government is permitted. Such a crabbed approach would clearly be pernicious in other settings where people commit themselves to a mixture of specific obligations and general principles, such as honor codes and wedding vows, and it has had an equally harmful effect on constitutionally limited government.

The idea that judges should strike down only those laws that are unambiguously prohibited by the Constitution represents a particularly stringent form of judicial restraint. As Judge Richard Posner explains, this version of judicial restraint "begins with an 1893 article by Harvard law professor James Bradley Thayer in which he argued that a statute should be invalidated only if its unconstitutionality is 'so clear that it is not open to rational question.'"[30] This hyperliteral approach to constitutional law was especially congenial to turn-of-the-century progressives, many of whom were legal positivists. In essence, positivism provides that there are no transcendent values, no such thing as natural rights or morality—or at least that those things, if they exist, are not a legitimate source of law. For positivists, law—including constitutional law—consists of whatever rules are explicitly written down and nothing else. Thus, positivism assumes that "statutes enacted by popularly-elected legislatures are law binding on judges, unless they violate an express prohibition in a popularly-enacted constitution."[31]

The progressive vision of government is of course much different from the Founders' vision. The Founders were mostly classical liberals who regarded natural rights and personal autonomy as preeminent values to which government poses a constant threat. Progressives tend to see government as a generally benevolent and effective tool for achieving particular outcomes, including a specific vision of social justice. In the early twentieth century, progressives were often quite statist, supporting everything from government price controls to eugenics and racial segregation.[32] Accordingly, they were typically hostile toward robust judicial review, which they correctly perceived as an impediment to their agenda.

According to Judge Posner, Professor Thayer's vision of judicial restraint did not simply mean deferring to legislatures in cases of uncertainty. Instead, "Thayer wanted judges to place a thumb on the scale" in favor of government.[33] Posner claims there are no "Thayerians" on the Supreme Court today, which may be true in the strictest sense. But that does not mean today's Supreme Court justices or lower-court judges wholly reject the idea of putting a thumb on the government's side of the scale in constitutional cases. On the contrary, they do so all the time, and that approach is an integral feature of modern constitutional doctrine, as exemplified by the rational basis test.

Thus, the view that judges should not strike down laws unless they are unambiguously prohibited by the Constitution persists to this day. Judge Robert Bork seems to have inspired an entire generation of conservative judicial minimalists in this regard, with his scorn for unenumerated rights and his strong preference for majoritarianism. But modern conservatives who embrace Bork's philosophy should understand that his disdain for robust judicial review tracks the progressives' position nearly verbatim.[34] Indeed, the progressives' theory of reflexive judicial restraint was developed for the specific purpose of removing constitutional obstacles to their vision of government. I sometimes refer to the rational basis test as "Roosevelt basis review" to remind my conservative friends whose water they're carrying when they embrace that standard for reviewing economic regulations and the exercise of federal power.

Among the leading conservative exponents of judicial restraint today is J. Harvie Wilkinson III, a highly respected federal judge on the Fourth Circuit Court of Appeals. In a recent article criticizing the *Heller* gun decision and comparing it to *Roe v. Wade*, Judge Wilkinson argues that judges should "be modest in their ambitions and overrule the results of the democratic process *only where the constitution unambiguously commands it.*"[35] Judge Wilkinson presents an eloquent, though I believe fundamentally flawed, argument for this proposition in his book *Cosmic Constitutional Theory: Why Americans Are Losing Their Inalienable Right to Self-Governance.* His position has many adherents, especially among conservatives, who tend to see it as a healthy antidote to the perceived excesses of the Warren Court.[36]

But for courts to do nothing unless the Constitution "unambiguously" commands otherwise is a recipe for more government, pure and simple. Constitutions are not designed to provide that level of detail, and furthermore, what counts as an "unambiguous" command turns out to be highly subjective. Judge Wilkinson, for example, does not believe the Second Amendment unambiguously protects an individual right to own guns, and he would have upheld Washington D.C.'s gun ban notwithstanding the amendment's plain statement that "the right of the people to keep and bear Arms, shall not be infringed."[37] And even the First Amendment, with its seemingly clear command that "Congress shall make no law . . . abridging the freedom of speech," has spawned disagreement about whether it applies to advertisements, flag burning, pornography, computer code, student speech, so-called "fighting words," election-related speech, or money used to facilitate election-related speech. As Professor Kermit Roosevelt has noted—and as any constitutional litigator knows very well—"the words of the Constitution alone seldom decide difficult cases."[38]

Another problem with the idea that courts should strike down laws only when the Constitution unambiguously commands it is that most judges are former lawyers, and lawyers are trained to find ambiguity in *anything*. The Constitution says the president has to be at least thirty-five years old. But what if we start colonizing other planets? It may seem obvious that the Constitution means thirty-five Earth years, although it doesn't say so. I suspect that at least some of the Framers felt the meaning of the Second Amendment was equally obvious.

And what about provisions that are less specific? As explained in the preceding chapter, the Fourteenth Amendment was designed to empower the federal government, and particularly the courts, to protect individual rights from tyrannical state and local governments in the wake of the Civil War. It is among the most important amendments to the Constitution, and its first command is that "[n]o state shall make or enforce any law which shall abridge the privileges or immunities of citizens of the United States."[39] This provision may be difficult to understand, but the fact that its framers chose to use broad language instead of creating a bullet-point list of prohibitions (which would have been impossible given the breadth and ingenuity of the misconduct at issue) provides no warrant to ignore it. Yet that is what the Supreme Court has done, a result that the self-proclaimed textualist Robert Bork tried to rationalize by suggesting that the privileges or immunities clause is so obscure it is as if that part of the Constitution had been covered up with an "ink blot." Judge Bork claims that the clause "has been a mystery since its adoption and in consequence has, quite properly, remained a dead letter."[40] But in fact there is a mass of historical evidence to illuminate the privileges or immunities clause, and while its *precise* meaning is debatable, just like most other constitutional provisions, the notion that it might as well have been written in Sanskrit, as Judge Bork suggests, is simply incorrect. There is a difference between being genuinely unable to understand a given constitutional provision and not even bothering to try.[41]

The Constitution is necessarily imprecise on many points. But imprecise doesn't mean silent. A student who acted as though everything not specifically forbidden by an honor code were permitted would be a cheat, as would a spouse who did everything not specifically forbidden by a wedding vow. It's the same with government. For the Constitution to serve its proper function, judges must give substance to every provision, not just the easy ones.

CHAPTER 7

The Judicial Activism
Bogeyman

Government has slipped its constitutional leash. It is voracious in
its pursuit and acquisition of power. "Between 1968 and 1978,"
one scholar notes, "Congress passed more regulatory legislation in a
decade than it had done in the whole prior history of the nation," and
that was well before it really hit its stride.[1] The federal government
makes little pretense of limiting itself to its constitutionally enumerated
powers, and the number of things that require government permission—whether it's going for a drive, drinking a Big Gulp, or chopping
down a tree in your own back yard—seems to grow every year.

And yet to hear pundits and politicians tell it, one of our nation's
biggest problems is "activist" judges making up rights and imposing
limits on government that aren't really in the Constitution. To the
contrary, isn't it painfully clear that under-enforcement of constitutional limits on government power is a far greater threat to America
than over-enforcement? If we want judges to be more serious about
enforcing those limits, then we've got to stop accusing them of activism
every time they say no to government.

People seem conflicted. On the one hand, most are fed up with
government and believe, correctly, that we have too much of it. But
many of those people also embrace the caricature of an activist judiciary inventing rights out of whole cloth and imposing nonexistent
limits on government power. But we don't have an activist judiciary. Not

remotely. What we have is an inconsistently engaged judiciary whose response to overweening government has been to meekly pledge ever greater deference to the "judgment" of politicians. But that supposed judgment is often no more than a polite fiction that credits government with more wisdom, better motives, and a greater self-restraint than it actually displays.

When people complain about activist judges being insufficiently deferential to the other branches, what they're really saying is that courts should generally allow politicians to decide how much power the Constitution gives politicians. That's a terrible idea, and we've had far too much of it over the past seventy-five years, ever since the Supreme Court gave away the farm (literally and figuratively) to the New Dealers in 1937. It's time for courts to get serious about constitutionally limited government again. But in order for that to happen, we've got to tone down the rhetoric about judicial activism.

WHAT IS "JUDICIAL ACTIVISM"?

When people accuse judges of activism, they rarely say exactly what they mean by that term. You have to figure it out from context. Usually the context is that a court has declared unconstitutional a particular law or policy that the accuser happens to like. And the accuser is not just saying the judge made a mistake. Instead, the charge of judicial activism includes a charge of bad faith—of deliberately misreading the Constitution to advance the judge's own policy preferences.

Though judicial activism is seldom defined, there seems to be a broad consensus that it's a genuine and serious problem. There are dozens of books about it, including bestsellers like Mark Levin's *Men in Black*. Controversial court decisions are routinely denounced as "activist" by people who don't like the results.[2] And some people even accuse the courts of perpetuating "judicial tyranny" through activist decisions.[3]

So what do people mean when they accuse judges of activism? Three basic points stand out: (1) the decision was not just wrong but indisputably wrong; (2) it was motivated by a desire to further the judge's personal policy preferences; and (sometimes) (3) it is part of a larger effort by judges of that stripe to promote a particular ideology.

Furthermore, though people sometimes accuse courts of activism for upholding government action, as when the Supreme Court authorized the use of eminent domain in *Kelo*, the charge is most often used to criticize courts for *blocking* government action, as the Court did when it struck down Washington D.C.'s handgun ban in *District of Columbia v. Heller*[4] and portions of the McCain-Feingold Act in *Citizens United*.[5] Lino Graglia, a University of Texas law professor and a strident critic of robust judicial review, speaks for many when he defines judicial activism as "the practice by judges of disallowing policy choices by other government officials or institutions that the Constitution does not clearly prohibit."[6] Notably, when it comes to federal powers, Professor Graglia's definition of activism turns the Constitution on its head. He assumes that all powers are permitted "that the Constitution does not clearly prohibit." Yet the Framers intended just the opposite: Powers are forbidden to the federal government unless they are enumerated and delegated in the Constitution.

Is there such a thing as judicial activism? Sure. Much as we hope they would not, some judges appear to have decided cases based on their personal policy preferences instead of the law. So it's not quite right to say judicial activism is a myth.[7] A better term is "bogeyman," which Wikipedia helpfully defines as "an amorphous imaginary being used by adults to frighten children into compliant behavior."[8] It's a neat fit because judicial activism, while not wholly imaginary, is an amorphous concept often used to browbeat judges into compliant behavior.

POLITICIANS PREFER JUDGES WHO AGREE TO PLAY BALL
Politicians tend to be some of the most vocal critics of judicial activism. President Obama claimed it would be a "good example" of judicial activism if the Supreme Court struck down his signature health-care

law. He said this just days after oral arguments at the Supreme Court revealed gaping holes in the administration's legal case and despite a Gallup poll showing that 71 percent of Americans believed the law was unconstitutional.[9] And yet the president claimed it would be not only wrong for the Supreme Court to strike down Obamacare, but "activist."

Politicians wield power, and judges enforce constitutional limits on that power. It's hardly surprising that they would have differing views on the contours of those limits, nor should we be surprised if politicians prefer judges who take a narrow view of their role. As a result, the judicial activism bogeyman stalks Capitol Hill during every high-profile judicial confirmation. Senators and staffers work late into the night before hearings, poring through files and fine-tuning questions designed to smoke out nominees who might be too aggressive about limiting government power. Indeed, transcripts of recent confirmation hearings suggest that no single issue more occupies the legislative mind during these proceedings than reining in "activist" judges. Particularly in the case of Supreme Court nominees, it appears that producing a more docile judiciary has become a major goal of the confirmation process.

Hearings begin with statements from members of the Senate Judiciary Committee, who often take the opportunity to express their concerns (and perhaps also try to shape public perception) about how the judiciary is doing its job. The theme that most often dominates those opening statements these days is judicial activism. But the term itself is rarely defined with any precision, and the existence of the problem is assumed, not demonstrated.

Let's start at the very top of the judicial branch. The chief justice of the United States is the leader of the federal judiciary and the first among equals on the Supreme Court. There have been only seventeen in the nation's history, and given the influence of the position, the stakes in the appointment process are enormous. So what did members of the Senate Judiciary Committee particularly focus on the last time a chief justice was nominated to the Supreme Court? Activism, restraint, and deference.

The transcript of John Roberts's 2005 confirmation hearing is replete with references to the supposed problem of judicial activism and the need for judges to be more "modest" about enforcing constitutional limits on government power. "Decades of judicial activism" have created "huge rifts in the social fabric of our country," according to one senator.[10] "Activism by a growing number of judges threatens our judiciary," claimed another senator.[11] Still another said that many Americans "fear our court is making policy when it repeatedly strikes down laws passed by elected members of Congress and elected members of state legislatures."[12] Roberts was then praised for having taken the position, during one of his many interviews with senators before the confirmation hearing, that "we need a more modest" Supreme Court.[13] Indeed, when asked about his judicial philosophy—whether he considered himself an originalist, strict constructionist, fundamentalist, etc.—he explained: "Like most people, I resist the labels. I have told people, when pressed, that I prefer to be known as a modest judge."[14] Over and over, Roberts emphasized his modesty, his humility, and his commitment to restraint. That is certainly admirable from one perspective; but from another, it appears dangerously close to unilateral disarmament by the judiciary.

And it has been the same thing with each Supreme Court nominee since then, particularly the most recent one, Elena Kagan. During the course of Kagan's nomination hearing, most of the senators' statements included discussions of judicial activism, though their particular definitions and examples varied depending on their political leanings.[15] Senators also grilled Kagan on her understanding of activism and modesty. For example, Senator Lindsey Graham asked Kagan to define the characteristics of an activist judge and to name a person, living or dead, who could be considered an activist judge.[16] Senator John Cornyn distinguished between "traditional" and activist jurisprudence and said he felt it important to determine whether Kagan "would move the Court in a traditional or an activist direction."[17] Like Chief Justice Roberts before her, Kagan emphasized that her time spent working in other branches had impressed upon her that the role of Supreme Court justices "must also be a modest one, properly deferential to the decisions of the American people and their elected representatives."[18]

These passages were not cherry-picked to create a distorted impression of the confirmation process. On the contrary, transcripts of the last four hearings for Supreme Court nominees frequently mention "activism," "deference," "restraint," "modesty," and "humility." The following table summarizes the number of times these terms were used in a context where the point was clearly to emphasize the need for a more permissive judiciary:[19]

Term	Roberts	Alito	Sotomayor	Kagan
Activist/ Activism	34	22	54	103
Defer/ Deference	20	38	45	55
Restrain/ Restrained/ Restraint	45	27	20	22
Modest/ Modesty	43	14	13	22
Humble/ Humility	13	3	13	11

So this seems to be the confirmation process in a nutshell: Senators start by asserting that activist judges have been encroaching on their turf and then ask the nominee what she will do about that problem *if* they decide to confirm her as a judge. Plainly there can be only one acceptable response, and it is the one dutifully given by every Supreme Court nominee for the past generation: fulsome assurances of modesty, restraint, and deference.

It's like a kid choosing his own babysitter: "As you know, whoever is ultimately confirmed for the position of new babysitter will be responsible for enforcing certain household rules, including how much candy I can eat, when I go to bed, and whether I can surf the Internet without a filter. Unfortunately, there's been a lot of activism in the enforcement of those rules lately, and I'm looking for more humility—a suitably modest and restrained babysitter who will defer to my understanding of the rules that apply in this house."

The analogy may seem flippant, but perhaps it's not so far off the mark. Parents hire babysitters even when children are perfectly capable of understanding household rules because children often push the bounds of those rules and sometimes ignore them altogether. Even good kids struggle with impulse control and have a tendency to rationalize their way around impediments to instant gratification. An institution that has racked up a national debt of more than $16 trillion with no sign of letting up has little room to complain about being compared to a child who eats too much candy or stays up past his bedtime.

Lest there be any doubt whether politicians use the judicial activism bogeyman to browbeat judges and would-be judges into compliant behavior, just read some of the transcripts from recent confirmation hearings and see whether that isn't precisely the subtext of the exchanges between senators and nominees. Consider this statement from Arlen Specter, chairman of the Senate Judiciary Committee, during Justice Alito's confirmation hearing:

> There is reason to believe that our Senate confirmation hearings may be having an effect on Supreme Court nominees on their later judicial duties. . . . In this process, nominees get an earful. While no promises are extracted, statements are made by nominees which may well influence their future decisions. Chief Justice Roberts, for example, will have a tough time giving a jolt to the system after preaching modesty and stability.[20]

Compare Senator Specter's assurance in 2006 that "no promises are extracted" from judicial nominees with his critique in 2010 of the *Citizens United* decision, in which he accused the Supreme Court of "eating Congress's lunch by invalidating legislation with judicial activism after nominees *commit under oath* in confirmation proceedings to respect Congressional fact finding and precedents." According to Specter, "Chief Justice Roberts and Justice Alito *repudiated their confirmation testimony* and provided the key votes" to strike down portions of the McCain-Feingold Act. "Roberts *promised* to just call balls and strikes. Then he moved the bases."[21]

Do some senators believe that "promises are extracted" from nominees to be submissive and let the other branches police themselves for constitutional compliance? You be the judge.

A COURT THAT RARELY SAYS NO

Between Senator Specter's claim that the Supreme Court "has been eating Congress's lunch" with judicial activism and the Judiciary Committee's obsessive focus on that issue, one assumes it must be happening all the time—that activist judges are constantly blocking legitimate policymaking efforts of the other branches.

But wait a minute. Legislators are not infallible, and neither are bureaucrats or the administrative agencies they work for. They will sometimes enact unconstitutional laws and regulations. Assuming that judicial review is a legitimate institution, as most Americans do, then courts should be striking down at least some of those policies. In a perfect world, the percentage of laws and regulations struck down by courts would be identical to the percentage of unconstitutional laws and regulations enacted.

Extending Chief Justice Roberts's memorable judges-as-umpires analogy, imagine government as a baseball pitcher trying to hit the constitutional strike zone as it makes and enforces laws. Major league pitchers throw strikes about 62 percent of the time.[22] Would we expect government officials to do better? In other words, if governing were a sport, how often would we expect legislators and bureaucrats to hit the constitutional strike zone with their policies and how often would they miss? Like pitchers, government officials sometimes have control problems, and, like pitchers, they have incentives to work the edges of the constitutional strike zone. So how often would we expect them to be on target? Half the time? Seventy-five percent? Ninety percent? More?

Between 1954 and 2002, Congress enacted 15,817 laws, of which the Supreme Court struck down 103—just 0.67 percent. The Court struck down an even smaller proportion of federal administrative regulations—about 0.5 percent—and a still smaller proportion of state laws: just 452 out of one million laws passed, or less than 0.05 percent. In any given year, the Supreme Court strikes down just three out of every five thousand state and federal laws passed.[23]

In light of history, experience, and common sense, it is implausible to suppose the federal government hits the constitutional strike zone 99.5 percent of the time. And yet the Supreme Court's strike-down rate for the past half-century is just 0.5 percent of all federal laws and regulations enacted. By that measure, the Supreme Court isn't eating Congress's lunch, as Senator Specter claimed; it's barely sweeping up the crumbs.[24]

But perhaps it's a mistake to focus on the percentage of laws struck down. Maybe when the Supreme Court declares a law unconstitutional it does so in a way that has the effect of taking down many other laws by implication or otherwise placing off-limits some entire area of policymaking.

There is scant evidence to support that premise. On the contrary, the Supreme Court has been increasingly inclined to resolve constitutional cases on an "as applied" basis, which results in narrower holdings limited to the particular facts of a given case. Moreover, in vast areas of public policy, courts apply no meaningful scrutiny to government regulation at all. Thus, federal and state governments enjoy essentially unfettered discretion in the areas of tax policy, business regulation, property ownership, land use, and myriad other fields involving constitutional values the Supreme Court considers nonfundamental.

In light of substantial evidence of judicial abdication—including widespread use of the rational basis test to rubber-stamp government action, open disregard for economic liberty and property rights, and the failure to enforce any serious concept of enumerated federal powers—those who claim that judicial activism is a serious problem bear a heavy burden of persuasion. But as Kermit Roosevelt explains in his excellent book *The Myth of Judicial Activism*, "the kinds of people who talk about judicial activism tend to make very little effort to explain *how* a decision conflicts with [the] plain meaning" of the Constitution.[25] What they offer instead is a mixture of anecdote and invective, criticizing court decisions that are based on perfectly defensible interpretations of the Constitution.

When the Supreme Court is accused of "activism" for restricting government power, it nearly always has credible reasons for its decisions.[26] Those reasons may not persuade everyone, but that doesn't mean they are not credible. Reasonable people can and do disagree about precisely what limits the Constitution imposes on government. Characterizing a given decision as "activist" means it is so clearly and indisputably wrong that it could only be the result of bad faith.[27] Very few decisions truly warrant that charge, and it is no accident that charges of activism tend to be based more on emotion than logic. It is one thing to glibly condemn a decision as "activist"; it is quite another to support that charge with an argument that is coherent, consistent, and free of Judge Bork's rhetorical ink blots and other shortcuts.

ACTIVISM, FALSE MODESTY, AND JUDICIAL ABDICATION

Whether intentionally or unwittingly, critics of judicial activism help create the impression that courts have been too active in restraining government when in fact they have been far too passive. This pushes the national dialogue in exactly the wrong direction, at least for those who favor constitutionally limited government. It helps reinforce the belief, much in vogue now, that the greatest judicial virtue is reflexive deference to the other branches of government. To be confirmed, judicial nominees must embrace the false proposition that judicial activism is a serious national problem and that the country needs a more modest judiciary.

But is "modest" really the right word to describe judges who systematically deprive the Constitution of substance by refusing to enforce power-limiting provisions that do not meet their exacting standards of clarity and specificity? What if the Framers meant to create a federal government whose powers are truly "few and defined"?[28] What if the Ninth Amendment reflects a genuine conviction that the enumeration of some rights in the Constitution should not be understood to negate—either theoretically or practically—the existence of others?[29] And what if the privileges or immunities clause of the Fourteenth Amendment was meant to do something important—isn't it incumbent on us to figure out what?[30]

Congress has been making a mockery of the Framers' plan for constitutionally limited government for the past seventy-five years. The Supreme Court has rendered practically meaningless some of the Constitution's most important and explicit protections of liberty. As a result, federal, state, and local officials are routinely allowed to impose on us in ways the Constitution was designed to prevent. At all levels, government is bigger, more intrusive, and less accountable than ever before. And yet the perception of an "activist" judiciary persists, demanding greater restraint in the face of other branches that have shown anything but.

A couple of years ago, I participated in a debate about judicial engagement at a law school on the East Coast. During the question-and-answer period, a retired state supreme court justice, who was serving as a visiting professor, objected to the idea of judges enforcing unenumerated rights on the usual ground that it is fundamentally antidemocratic and gives judges too much discretion to interfere in the results of the political process. Following the event, I approached the judge to thank him for his questions and ask by way of follow-up whether he would enforce a constitutional amendment that said something like: "We the people of the United States, having carefully considered the pros and cons of empowering judges to enforce unenumerated natural rights of American citizens, hereby instruct them to do so." He said he would refuse to enforce such an amendment. With all due respect, that isn't modesty; it's abdication.

CHAPTER 8

Real Judging in All Constitutional Cases

Judicial engagement is a truly modest proposal. It means real judging in *all* constitutional cases. The fateful error into which modern constitutional law has fallen—the notion that we should have genuine judging in some cases and make-believe judging in others—makes the concept of judicial engagement seem radical to people who favor the current approach. But it's really not.

By calling for real judging in all constitutional cases instead of a select handful, proponents of judicial engagement emphatically reject the myths of majoritarianism and the bullet-point Constitution. Instead, judicial engagement embraces the idea that the powers of government are limited, that they may be used to restrict people's freedom only for a valid reason, and that these powers should be exercised with at least a modicum of care. As a result, the government must justify its actions to the people, not the other way around.

At a minimum, real judging in all cases means:

- *Neutrality.* Judges should not serve as advocates by inventing justifications for government action or rewriting laws that don't measure up.
- *Consistency.* In all cases, not just some, judges should candidly seek to determine what ends the government is pursuing and

ensure that both its ends and its means are constitutionally legitimate.

- *No free passes.* Facts matter in all cases. Judges should not accept as true any contested factual assertions for which the government has no evidence.
- *Burden of proof.* Government must demonstrate the need for any interference with constitutionally secured rights.

GOVERNMENT-CENTRIC CONSTITUTIONAL LAW

Medieval astronomers committed a fundamental error that made it impossible for them to reconcile their mathematical calculations with their observations of planetary motion: they put Earth at the center of the solar system instead of the sun. Modern constitutional law makes the same mistake by putting government at the center of the constitutional cosmos instead of the individual. Thus, where medieval astronomers invented exotic concepts like epicycles to explain why Mars sometimes appears to move backward in its orbit,[1] our courts have invented doctrines like the rational basis test and the aggregation principle in order to empower government in ways the Constitution was designed to prevent.

But modern constitutional law's conception of a government-centric Constitution—meaning a system in which government action is generally presumed valid and individuals must justify their exercise of liberty—is fundamentally inconsistent with the Framers' vision. The Framers understood very well that government sometimes pursues legitimate ends, like protecting citizens from criminals or foreign aggression, and sometimes pursues illegitimate ends, like silencing critics or playing favorites in the marketplace. There is nothing to suggest that the Framers intended a system in which courts would block the illegitimate exercise of government power in some cases while rationalizing it in others. But that's what constitutional law has become.

CUTTING-EDGE JUDGING

We have seen the radically different ways that courts approach fundamental rights, which get genuine judicial review, and nonfundamental rights, which do not. To better appreciate the difference between abdication and engagement, let's look at a cutting-edge issue where the Supreme Court has not yet weighed in: recording the actions of police officers in public places.

More and more people are doing it, often in the face of strong resistance. Some states even have laws against recording people without their permission, including public officials. In Illinois, for example, it's a felony to record a conversation without the consent of all parties, and if one of them is a law enforcement officer then it's a class one felony with a prison sentence of up to fifteen years. There have been numerous prosecutions.[2]

Can the government really put people in jail for recording police officers in public, or is there a constitutional right to do it? And if there is a right, is it a fundamental right subject to meaningful judicial protection, or a nonfundamental right to which the rubber-stamp, "rationalize-a-basis" test applies? The Supreme Court hasn't answered these questions yet, but they are working their way through the lower courts. It's a fascinating issue that could affect anyone who carries a smartphone—which is to say, just about everyone.

When police interact with civilians in the line of duty, the stakes can be enormous on both sides. Police officers are vested with substantial powers, both official and unofficial, and regrettably those powers are sometimes abused. For their part, police have a difficult job in which they routinely encounter people at their worst: violent, desperate, impaired, and often with something to hide. It is clear that both police and civilians have been victimized by inaccurate and sometimes deliberately false accounts of their interactions with one another. Until recently, it was almost always a question of one side's word against the other's. Not anymore.

Most everyone has seen footage from police dashboard cameras, and police have long used a variety of devices, both openly and secretly, to record their interactions with citizens. But with the advent of smartphones and other personal recording devices, it is increasingly common for civilians to turn the tables. Some officers try to discourage this, even to the point of arresting people on catchall charges like disorderly conduct, or simply taking the recording device and deleting or destroying its contents.[3] In states that specifically prohibit recording people without their permission, nearly all prosecutions have been for recording public officials, not fellow civilians.[4]

Prohibiting people from recording the public actions of government officials raises a host of constitutional concerns, including a free-speech right to gather and disseminate information under the First Amendment,[5] unreasonable search and seizure under the Fourth Amendment,[6] and a due process right to collect and preserve evidence under the Fifth and Fourteenth Amendments.[7] And while the Supreme Court has not yet resolved the issue, the clear trend in the lower courts has been in favor of recognizing a constitutional right to record the actions of government officials, including police officers, in public.[8]

Deciding whether there is a constitutional right to record government officials in public—and if so, whether to characterize that right as fundamental or nonfundamental—requires careful thought. There is of course nothing in the text of the Constitution about smartphones or video cameras, nor is it clear that the First Amendment's protection of free speech and the press covers nonjournalists making recordings. On the other hand, most people do not view the Constitution as some ancient relic, unable to bridge the gap from quill pens and printing presses to iPhones and the Internet. The use of technology to make accurate records of public proceedings is something the Framers would certainly have appreciated as an aid to political accountability. That doesn't necessarily mean the Constitution protects it, but the values at stake are clearly ones the Framers cared about.

Illinois has been so aggressive about enforcing its "eavesdropping" law against people for recording police officers that the ACLU launched a test case to challenge the law in federal court. The trial judge dismissed the case on the premise that the Constitution provides no protection for recording police officers in public. In May 2012, a divided panel of the Seventh Circuit Court of Appeals reversed that decision and enjoined the state from enforcing the ban. The majority and dissenting opinions in *ACLU v. Alvarez* are a perfect study in the difference between judicial engagement and judicial abdication.

Describing the state's position as "extreme" and "extraordinary," Judge Diane Sykes firmly rejected the idea that the First Amendment provides no protection at all for making recordings simply because recording devices are not specifically mentioned in the text.[9] After all, the Supreme Court has held that movies are a protected form of speech, and according to Judge Sykes, "[t]he act of *making* an audio or audiovisual recording is . . . a corollary of the right to disseminate the resulting recording."[10] Since a major purpose of the First Amendment was to protect people's ability to discuss government affairs, being able to record those affairs accurately has obvious constitutional significance.[11]

As for the state's assertion that it was trying to protect "conversational privacy," Judge Sykes zeroed in on a glaring inconsistency. The statute was designated as an "eavesdropping" law, but the state conceded that it does not prohibit people from *listening* to a police officer's public conversations or photographing or transcribing them by hand. Instead, the law makes it a felony to audio-record those same conversations even when they are not in fact private, but are audible to the person making the recording and anyone within earshot may lawfully listen to them.[12] There is simply no good reason for making it a crime to *record* public conversations that people have every right to listen to if they wish.

Judge Richard Posner dissented. Judge Posner is one of the nation's best-known judges and a prolific writer off the bench, whose forty books run the gamut from economics and antitrust law to one called *Sex and Reason.*[13] Few judges have exercised their First Amendment right of free speech more broadly, more vigorously, or more creatively than Judge Posner. And yet his opinion supporting the government's power to imprison people for up to fifteen years just for recording public conversations of law enforcement officers gives incredibly short shrift to the values underlying that provision.

Without assessing the nature of the right at stake (i.e., fundamental or nonfundamental), Judge Posner begins with the premise that the playing field should be sharply tilted in favor of government. In his view, "[t]he invalidation of a statute on constitutional grounds should be a rare and solemn judicial act, done with reluctance under compulsion of clear binding precedent or clear constitutional language or—in the absence of those traditional sources of guidance—compelling evidence, or an overwhelming gut feeling, that the statute has intolerable consequences."[14] This statement is worth parsing.

First, why should the invalidation of a statute necessarily be a "rare" judicial act? Ideally, the number of laws struck down by courts should match the number of unconstitutional laws passed by legislatures. It is unclear whether Judge Posner is making an empirical assertion—i.e., that legislatures rarely pass unconstitutional laws and therefore courts will rarely have occasion to strike them down—or a normative one, namely, that courts should rarely strike down unconstitutional legislation no matter how much of it comes down the pike. Either way, the idea that judges should "rarely" declare laws unconstitutional seems no more sound than the idea that NFL referees should "rarely" call penalties for holding or pass interference. Whenever there's a foul, that's when a penalty should be called—whether in football or in politics.

And the idea that judges should strike down laws with "reluctance" seems equally loaded. Should radiologists be reluctant to tell us what they really see on an MRI? How about aircraft maintenance engineers—should they take an airplane out of service only with "reluctance," or should they simply call it like they see it and let the chips fall where they may?

As for the "compulsion of clear binding precedent" or "clear constitutional language," these too are loaded terms that create a presumption of legitimacy in the government's favor. Likewise, the requirement to present "compelling evidence . . . that the statute has intolerable consequences" sets up a nearly insurmountable obstacle for anyone challenging a law.

According to Judge Posner, then, the government bears no obligation to justify a policy that would put people in jail for up to fifteen years for recording a public conversation. Instead, the burden rests entirely on those who feel they should not be imprisoned for making an accurate record of a conversation taking place right in front of them. The idea that people must justify their actions to the government and not the other way around is certainly one view of government, but it is not the one embodied in our Constitution. As James Madison explained, "[a]n *elective despotism* was not the government we fought for."[15]

But perhaps most striking of all—and a persistent feature of judicial abdication—is Judge Posner's failure to squarely address the government's true ends. Illinois's eavesdropping law is the broadest of its kind in the nation. No other state "prohibits the open recording of police officers lacking any expectation of privacy."[16] Neither the state's lawyers nor Judge Posner cites any evidence that such recordings have caused problems in other jurisdictions, nor does Judge Posner examine the enforcement history of the Illinois law to see whether it is consistent with the state's asserted goal of protecting legitimate privacy interests.

Instead of looking at context and evidence to draw what should be fairly obvious conclusions about the state's true ends in prosecuting people for recording public interactions between police and civilians, Judge Posner extols the importance of privacy as a "social value" and frets about officers' ability to stay focused on their work in the presence of anyone with a smartphone or other recording device. He worries that an officer may "freeze" if he sees a journalist recording his conversation with a suspect or a potential witness.[17] Suffice it to say that police in Chicago, where Judge Posner's courthouse is located, do not have a reputation as shrinking violets who cringe before reporters and camera-wielding civilians.

No, this law is not about protecting the delicate sensibilities of easily flustered police officers. It's about government controlling the narrative, period. If you have any doubts, go on YouTube and type in "police assault" or "police brutality." You will see shocking examples of misconduct; so many that it is impossible to discount them all. It is perfectly clear why citizens would want to make their own record of these encounters, and it is equally clear why the officers involved might wish to prevent them from doing so. Judge Posner gives a perfunctory nod to the possibility that police officers might not always be candid about such incidents, but that forms no serious part of his analysis.[18]

Judge Posner's willingness to credit the government's implausible concerns about conversational privacy while paying virtually no attention to the very real problems of government accountability and misconduct is the very essence of judicial abdication. And holding that citizens must justify with "compelling evidence" the simple act of recording their interactions with law enforcement gets the constitutional prerogatives exactly backward. In America, the default setting is liberty, not regulation.

JUDICIAL ENGAGEMENT BY THE NUMBERS

Despite its modest plea that judges simply act like real judges in *all* constitutional cases instead of a favored few, judicial engagement strikes some people as revolutionary—perhaps even a veiled call for judicial activism. It isn't.

Americans are subject to a vast web of government regulation. Most of these regulations do not involve rights that courts recognize as "fundamental" and thus entitled to meaningful judicial protection. As a result, judges in most instances begin with an effectively predetermined outcome—that the government should be allowed to do whatever it is doing—and work their way backward from there. This approach ensures that government rarely has to justify its interference with liberty or demonstrate the legitimacy of its policies. It also enables courts to avoid giving a candid assessment of the other branches' conduct in most cases.

If there is anything revolutionary about the call for judicial engagement, it's the concept of requiring the government to justify its actions with honest explanations and credible evidence in all cases. While that would certainly be a significant change from the way constitutional law is practiced now, it is really a call for judicial *activity*, not activism.

Here are four principles of engaged judging:

1. *Figure out what the government is really up to.*

The first and most important question in any constitutional case is whether the government is pursuing a constitutionally legitimate end. Recall the earlier discussion about the constitutionality of recording police officers in public. A recent news story describes how a man in San Diego was using his smartphone to record a police officer who was giving him a ticket for smoking in public. The officer instructs the man to put the phone away. The man responds that he has a right to record the incident, and the police officer tells him he does not because "a cell phone can be converted into a weapon."[19] But the officer's conduct flatly belies his stated concern about the phone being used as a weapon: neither his actions nor his demeanor suggests that he feels any genuine threat to his or his partner's safety. Instead, it is plain that he simply doesn't wish to be recorded.

Or consider another recent example. Two brothers set off bombs at the Boston Marathon on April 15, 2013, killing three people and severely wounding dozens more. Police ordered people to stay in their homes during the ensuing manhunt. There is simply no way to judge the constitutionality of confining people to their homes in the abstract. If it's done to protect people from danger and assist law enforcement in capturing suspects in the immediate aftermath of a terrorist attack, that's one thing. But if it were done to prevent people from voting or attending a political rally, then it would be a completely different story.

The notion that it is categorically impossible to say what ends the government is actually pursuing in any given case is pernicious and false. How do we know? Because courts make that inquiry all the time in cases involving rights they deem worthy of meaningful protection.

Thus, when a law or policy is reviewed under any form of "heightened" (meaning real) scrutiny, the government must provide a "genuine" explanation for its actions, not one that has been "hypothesized or invented *post hoc* in response to litigation."[20] Unlike rational basis review, under heightened scrutiny "the mere recitation of a benign . . . purpose is not an automatic shield which protects against any inquiry into the *actual purposes* underlying a statutory scheme."[21] The government must demonstrate the legitimacy of its actions, and that burden "is not satisfied by mere speculation or conjecture."[22] Instead, the government must support its factual assertions with "actual, reliable evidence."[23] Courts will not permit the government to "get away with shoddy data or reasoning" where fundamental rights are at stake.[24] Instead, the evidence produced by the government must "fairly support" its asserted justification for the law, whatever that may be.[25]

But maybe it's possible to determine the government's true ends in some areas, like racial discrimination or the free exercise of religion, and impossible in other areas, like economic regulation. Wrong again. The Supreme Court recently confirmed that judges can and should evaluate the government's true ends in enforcing particular kinds of economic regulations. Thus, when a state treats its own citizens more favorably than citizens from other states in the economic sphere, the relevant inquiry is whether the laws were in fact "enacted for the protectionist purpose of burdening out-of-state citizens."[26] A classic case from 1948 involved a South Carolina law that charged residents $25 for a shrimping license and nonresidents $2,500. The Supreme Court found that the "purpose and effect" of the law was to "create a commercial monopoly for South Carolina residents"—not, as South Carolina claimed, simply to conserve shrimp—and struck the law down.[27] Indeed, in cases where it has struck down economic regulations that favor state residents over nonresidents, the Supreme Court has found that "*the clear aim of the statute* at issue was to advantage in-state workers and commercial interests at the expense of their out-of-state counterparts."[28] So it's not that courts are categorically unable to ascertain the government's true ends in cases involving economic regulations—it's that most of the time they simply don't bother to try.

Perhaps the Supreme Court has been deluding itself that it can identify the government's true ends in determining the validity of various laws, like ones that discriminate against women, minorities, or nonresidents. But that seems unlikely. Judges are actually quite good at ferreting out the truth, even when the government tries to hide it. That some constitutional cases should involve a genuine search for truth while others should not is a choice the Supreme Court has made. There is certainly nothing that compels that choice, and in my view there is not much to commend it either.

2. *Make them prove it.*

For regulation to be lawful, the government must be pursuing a constitutionally valid end using constitutionally permissible means. In making that determination, facts matter—real facts, that is, not ones that have been presumed, hypothesized, or conjured out of thin air. And because experience shows that government is not always candid regarding the factual basis for its actions, any constitutional doctrine that assumes otherwise is bound to result in serious injustices.

For example, in one of the most infamous cases of the twentieth century, *Korematsu v. United States*,[29] the Supreme Court upheld the constitutionality of an executive order authorizing the internment of Japanese Americans during World War II. The Court's ruling was largely based on the government's representations that it had evidence that some of those citizens were spies and saboteurs who represented a grave threat to national security. But by the time the case reached the Supreme Court, it was clear that those initial concerns were unfounded, and in fact the federal government was in possession of more recent reports that flatly contradicted its earlier position. Several Justice Department lawyers concluded that a key report on which the government had been relying in the litigation contained "lies" and "intentional falsehoods" that should have been disclosed to the Supreme Court.[30] They were overruled by their superiors, and the Supreme Court was never advised that the Justice Department seriously doubted the veracity of key "facts" upon which the government had built its case.[31] In short, the federal government deliberately misled the courts in defending the constitutionality of its wartime internment policy and got away with it.[32]

Unfortunately, the government's litigation misconduct in *Korematsu* was not an isolated event. On the contrary, *USA Today* recently conducted an exhaustive, six-month investigation into the issue of prosecutorial misconduct among lawyers of the Justice Department and found a pattern of "'serious, glaring misconduct'" that some experts believed represented only the "'tip of the iceberg.'"[33] While some incidents may be the result of inadvertence or error, it is clear that not all of them are. For example, in reviewing a drug conviction in 2006, one federal court of appeals concluded that a prosecutor's failure to disclose potentially exculpatory information "was designed to deliberately mislead the court and defense counsel."[34] Similarly, a recent editorial in the *New York Times* made a strong and well-documented argument that police officers in some jurisdictions routinely lie under oath to help obtain convictions and to support one another's stories about how events transpired.[35]

To be clear, this is not to suggest the government is more likely to mislead judges than private parties are. Instead, the point is simply that there is ample evidence that government officials are not always candid in court, and a constitutional doctrine that assumes otherwise—that simply accepts at face value the government's factual assertions the way the Supreme Court did in *Korematsu*—will necessarily produce significant errors and injustices.

3. *Don't help the government justify its actions.*

As mentioned in the chapter on judicial activism, Chief Justice Roberts famously observed during his confirmation hearing that "[j]udges are like umpires. . . . They make sure everybody plays by the rules."[36] Judges certainly should act like umpires, and in some constitutional cases they do. In rational basis cases, however, judges wear the uniform of an umpire at the same time they are charged with helping one team—the government—win the game. Recall that judges applying rational basis review are not only permitted but *obligated* to help think of justifications for a challenged law if the government's lawyers are not sufficiently creative to invent their own.[37] And in fact, judges sometimes do help the government by inventing justifications to support its actions in rational basis cases.

For example, in *FCC v. Beach Communications, Inc.*,[38] a federal law included "quasi-private" satellite systems within a particular regulation but not fully private ones. The result was to enable local governments to impose the same regulations on the "quasi-private" satellite systems as they did with cable television companies. A group of satellite companies challenged the regulation as creating an arbitrary distinction among similarly situated entities. At one stage in the proceedings, a judge on the D.C. Circuit Court of Appeals suggested that the Federal Communications Commission could have set the distinctions because an external, quasi-private satellite system was "similar" to cable, and the FCC conceded that it could offer no better rationale.[39] But the other two judges on the panel rejected the "impression of 'similarity'" as no more than "a naked intuition, unsupported by conceivable facts or policies."[40] The Supreme Court reversed and upheld the law, partly on the basis of the rationale suggested by the one appellate court judge and partly on the basis of new rationales, including one that appears to have been suggested by an unidentified justice during oral argument.[41]

Or consider *Armour v. City of Indianapolis*.[42] To finance a new sewer project, the City of Indianapolis allowed residents to pay their assessments all at once or in installments. One year later, the city changed the financing scheme and canceled the remaining installments for those homeowners who chose to pay over time, while refusing to refund a pro rata share to people who paid the full amount up front. As a result, some people ended up paying thirty times more than others for the same service.[43] The Indiana Supreme Court upheld the city's actions by inventing a number of hypothetical justifications that had not been offered by the city's attorneys. These included the court's surmise that the city could have believed that those who had paid up front were "in better financial positions" than those on the installment plan, or "that the benefits of simplifying sanitary sewer funding outweighed the effort of continuing a collection system for thousands of taxpayers."[44] The Supreme Court ultimately affirmed the decision on grounds of administrative convenience. There was no suggestion that the Indiana Supreme Court had done anything wrong by inventing justifications for the government's conduct out of whole cloth.[45]

4. *Put the burden of proof where it belongs.*

When government seeks to regulate, it must have a constitutionally valid reason for doing so. And in cases involving fundamental rights, courts put the burden of proving the existence of such a reason where it belongs: on the government. When you think about it, this is only fair; after all, the government presumably knows why it seeks to enforce a particular law or policy, and if it can't come up with any reason for doing so, then that's a pretty strong indication that the government's action is arbitrary. As Randy Barnett asks rhetorically in his book *Restoring the Lost Constitution*, "who . . . is in the best position to present a court with empirical information for or against the necessity of a statute: agencies of government who proposed it or an affected individual or company on whom it is imposed?"[46]

And yet, in cases involving nonfundamental rights, courts applying rational basis review place the burden of proof on the individual to show that the government has no good reason for its regulation. Sometimes called the "presumption of constitutionality," this approach gets the presumption exactly backward. In fact, courts seem perfectly aware that it does—at least in other settings. For example, one federal appeals court has noted that "[a] presumption is generally employed to benefit a party who does not have control of the evidence on an issue. . . . It would be unjust to employ a presumption to relieve a party of its burden of production when that party has all the evidence regarding that element of the claim."[47] In all constitutional cases, the government is in possession of the relevant information—namely, why it is enforcing a given law or policy—and therefore the burden of producing that information should be on the government in all cases, not just some. When government seeks to restrict our liberty, we should not be required to guess why.

JUDICIAL ENGAGEMENT MEANS REAL JUDGING IN ALL CASES

In striking down Obamacare's individual mandate in the decision that was later overruled by the Supreme Court, the Eleventh Circuit Court of Appeals said that when Congress oversteps the outer limits of its authority, "the Constitution requires judicial engagement, not judicial abdication."[48]

This is progress. It reflects an awareness of the problem and its antidote. It is also the first time a federal court has ever used the term "judicial engagement" as an antonym for abdication. Hopefully it will not be the last, because the need for robust judicial enforcement of constitutional limits on government power has never been more acute. Fortunately, there are other encouraging signs as well.

Since the 1930s, it has been practically impossible to get federal courts to subject economic regulations to any significant level of review. Courts have shown particular deference to occupational licensing laws, leaving government with practically unfettered authority to dictate who may work in which occupation, subject to what requirements. As with so many constitutional rights, the Supreme Court has long recognized that there is a right "to pursue any livelihood or avocation"[49] but has refused to provide any meaningful protection for it. Two cases involving the sale of caskets have bucked the trend of judicial abdication by doing something quite extraordinary in the context of economic liberty litigation: the judges refused to accept pretextual explanations for government regulation.

In a 2002 case called *Craigmiles v. Giles*, the Sixth Circuit Court of Appeals considered the constitutionality of a Tennessee law that allowed only state-licensed funeral directors to sell caskets. A casket, of course, is a large wooden or metal box; there is no good reason to restrict who may sell one, and in fact the vast majority of states do not. Nevertheless, the state's lawyers argued that the court should defer to the purely imaginary—and factually baseless—concerns the legislature might have had regarding public health and consumer protection.

Writing for a unanimous panel, Judge Danny Boggs recognized the great deference owed to legislatures under controlling Supreme Court precedent, and noted that even "foolish and misdirected" laws are generally found to be valid "if subject only to rational basis review."[50] Unlike most courts, however, the panel didn't stop there. Instead, it considered the possibility that economic protectionism might be the *only plausible* explanation for Tennessee's casket-sale restrictions; and protectionism, according to the Sixth Circuit's correct understanding of basic civics, is not a legitimate governmental purpose. The court systematically examined each of Tennessee's nonprotectionist explanations for the law—that it was trying to maintain public health and safety while preventing unscrupulous casket retailers from exploiting emotionally vulnerable customers, etc.—and found all of them to be utterly insupportable. These justifications, said the court, "come close to striking us with the force of a five-week-old, unrefrigerated dead fish, a level of pungence almost required to invalidate a statute under rational basis review."[51] For a government lawyer to present a court with an argument so rotten that it will not even pass muster under the almost infinitely forgiving rational basis test is something of an achievement, albeit a dubious one. But Louisiana managed to do just that eleven years later in a case involving an almost identical law against unlicensed casket sales that the state was trying to enforce against a bunch of monks, of all people.

The Benedictine monks of Saint Joseph Abbey, just outside New Orleans, support themselves and their monastery by making simple wooden caskets in their own workshop. They sell these caskets to the public, which is illegal in Louisiana because the monks are not state-licensed funeral directors.

As in Tennessee, Louisiana's lawyers tried to portray the law as a bona fide attempt to protect consumers from ignorant or unscrupulous casket retailers. And just as the Sixth Circuit did with Tennessee's law, the Fifth Circuit in *St. Joseph Abbey v. Castille* carefully evaluated each of Louisiana's proffered justifications for allowing only state-licensed funeral directors to sell caskets in order to determine whether any of them were truly plausible.[52] But those justifications simply could not withstand honest scrutiny. Among other things, the state-mandated training for funeral directors does not include instruction on selecting caskets, nor, contrary to the state's professed concerns, is any training required in dealing with grief-stricken customers.[53] Moreover, there is no requirement in Louisiana (or any other state, for that matter) to use a casket for the burial of human remains, nor does the state impose any requirements for the construction or design of caskets.[54] In other words, the state's asserted public policy justifications for the casket-sales requirement were transparently false. The only question was whether the court would go along with the charade and rubber-stamp the government's explanation for its nakedly anticompetitive licensing law, as courts normally do.

Not this time. The Fifth Circuit explained, "The great deference due state economic regulation does not demand judicial blindness to the history of a challenged rule or the context of its adoption nor does it require courts to accept nonsensical explanations for regulation."[55] Having rejected the state's unsupported, implausible, and palpably insincere justifications for its casket-sales law, the court observed, "The funeral directors have offered no rational basis for their challenged rule and, try as we are required to do, we can suppose none."[56]

Contrast those rulings with that of the Tenth Circuit Court of Appeals in a 2004 case called *Powers v. Harris*, involving a nearly identical challenge to Oklahoma's casket-sales law.[57] In upholding the law, the court recited the familiar rational basis language to the effect that the ends the state was actually pursuing were "entirely irrelevant," as was the complete lack of empirical evidence supporting the legislature's policy choice.[58] Accordingly, the court had to consider every "plausible" basis for the law, including simple economic protectionism for the local funeral industry. Incredibly, two judges on the panel held that "intrastate economic protectionism"—literally favoring one group of people over another—is a legitimate basis for restricting the constitutional rights of the disfavored group. As the two judges explained, "while baseball may be the national pastime of the citizenry, dishing out special economic benefits to certain in-state industries remains the favored pastime of state and local governments."[59] That may well be, but only because the federal judiciary has been asleep at the switch for decades. Whether intentionally or not, the panel's flippant attitude toward naked economic protectionism perfectly reflects the constitutional doctrine they applied in approving it.

The significance of the *Craigmiles* and *St. Joseph Abbey* decisions cannot be overstated. Together with a 2008 pest-control case from California,[60] they represent the only times in seventy-five years that federal appellate courts have subjected occupational licensing laws to meaningful scrutiny and squarely confronted the demonstrably illegitimate governmental purposes behind them. That is the epitome of judicial engagement, or, as we might say even more simply, real judging. America needs a lot more of it.

* * *

Constitutional limits on government power are meaningless without judges to enforce them. The choice between improper judicial activism and supposedly laudable judicial restraint is a false one. The real choice is either consistent, conscientious judging in all cases, or a system where some judges sometimes make a genuine effort to ensure that the government is acting constitutionally, while others simply bury their heads in the sand to avoid seeing what the government is really doing. Striking down unconstitutional laws and blocking illegitimate government actions is not judicial activism; it is judicial *engagement*—enforcing limits on government power consistent with the text, purpose, and history of the Constitution.

CHAPTER 9

From Abdication to Engagement

The Constitution imposes substantial limits on government power. Our judiciary, for the most part, does not. As that disconnect grows, so does government. And the bigger government gets, the less room people have to make their own decisions about everything from supporting causes of their own choosing, to earning a living and enjoying the comforts of home. Even when government means well, it tends to impose one-size-fits-all solutions to problems that are better addressed through individual initiative, creativity, and compassion. Regrettably, government does not always mean well, and it is not always candid about its true ends or the means used to achieve them.

Americans are entitled to the full measure of freedom the Constitution provides for them. Reasonable people may differ about just how much freedom that is and precisely what limits the Constitution imposes on government. But the need for courts to enforce those limits if they are to mean anything is inarguable. Without a properly engaged judiciary, we are left to rely on the self-restraint of public officials, which experience has shown amounts to no restraint at all. As Professor Richard Epstein notes, "it is not possible to marry any conception of limited constitutional governance with large doses of judicial passivity."[1] He's absolutely right about that, as we have learned to our cost.

So what can we do?

There are no easy answers, and I certainly will not suggest otherwise. But there is cause for optimism about the prospects for constitutionally limited government in America. The Supreme Court touched a nerve in the national psyche when it ruled in *Kelo v. City of New London* that government may take a law-abiding citizen's home and give it to someone else in the mere hope that the new owner will put the property to more valuable use. When Obamacare's individual mandate was challenged in court, polls showed that a clear majority of Americans—including many who actually supported the law on policy grounds—believed it to be an unconstitutional exercise of federal power.[2] And when I give talks and participate in debates at law schools, which I do frequently, I find that law students quickly grasp how fundamentally unjust the rational basis test is as a standard of review for protecting constitutional rights.

Here I offer three suggestions for how we might foster a more engaged judiciary. First, supporters of limited government should make clear that a ritual pledge of modesty, restraint, and deference toward other branches is not what they expect from judicial nominees. Instead, a judge's confirmation should depend substantially on his or her ability to articulate a concrete theory of limited government. Second, we should not allow our attitude toward judicial review to be driven by one or two hot-button issues, as unfortunately happens today. And third, we must understand that we have no inherent right to impose our will on other people. It may be permissible to do so when there is a constitutionally valid reason. But there is nothing to fear or resent about submitting that question to a neutral arbiter if we wish to bring the coercive power of law to bear on people who disagree with our own policy preferences.

A FRESH TAKE ON JUDICIAL NOMINATIONS

Each of the last four confirmation hearings for Supreme Court nominees has focused heavily on the supposed problem of judicial activism, with "activism" being a transparent code word for judges saying no to government. The tacit assumption appears to be that even though the Supreme Court has struck down less than 0.5 percent of all federal laws enacted in the past fifty years and less than 0.05 percent of state laws, it is still being far too aggressive in enforcing constitutional limits on government. This approach to confirming justices needs to change. Confirmation hearings should spend at least as much time focusing on the "activism" of legislative and executive branch officials, who have scarcely been models of restraint in their own exercise of power. Granted, most senators probably do not wish to hear from a judicial nominee that Congress routinely exercises powers not delegated to it by the Constitution, and a president may feel understandably reluctant to appoint judges who do not take for granted that the current alphabet soup of federal agencies and programs is fully constitutional. So it is incumbent on those of us who want fewer regulations, who believe the Constitution provides for less government than we have today, to insist on judicial nominees who share these views and will not allow themselves to be buffaloed by legislators who believe, absurdly, that a serious national problem is judges interpreting the Constitution in a way that gives the other branches too little room to operate.

I realize that there are formidable challenges to getting a critical mass of judges appointed to the courts who are prepared to acknowledge that the status quo is fundamentally at odds with our Constitution as it was designed to work. The process by which judges are nominated and confirmed is fundamentally political, and most politicians are not looking for ways to clip their own wings. But there are some real bright spots in the judiciary today, both federal and state. I have met engaged judges, I have appeared before them, and I had the great honor of working for one after law school. My respect and admiration for their commitment to principle is boundless. But we need more judges like these, and we need them soon.

Confirmation hearings provide an important opportunity to educate the public about how well the judiciary is fulfilling its constitutional role

151

as a check on government. I believe the lesson could be driven home with great effect if even one or two senators focused as much on judicial abdication during their questioning as other senators do on judicial activism. Of course, one of the perennial challenges in confirmation hearings is the tendency of nominees to duck hard questions and avoid giving concrete answers by invoking the duty to refrain from committing to a specific position in any case that might come before them as a sitting judge.[3] But an adroit questioner—and there are some very good ones on the Senate Judiciary Committee right now—can push back against that sort of intransigence and, at the very least, make a good deal of hay with a nominee's persistent refusal to provide clear answers to fair but difficult questions. Here are some I would like to see asked.

- Do you believe the powers of the federal government were meant to be "few and defined," as James Madison wrote in *Federalist* 45? Would it be accurate to describe the powers of the federal government today as "few and defined"?
- Could you identify which constitutional provisions you believe impose significant limits on government power and explain how?
- Are there any cases in which the Supreme Court erred by granting the federal government more power than the Constitution does? If so, should those decisions be reversed?
- Do you believe there are any federal agencies whose existence may not be authorized by the Constitution?
- In some constitutional cases, courts require a "genuine" explanation for the government's actions and judge the constitutionality of those actions based on the government's true ends. Do you believe there should be a class of cases in which courts ignore the government's true ends and invite the government to offer explanations for its conduct that are hypothetical instead of genuine?
- Do you believe judges should help the government prevail in constitutional cases by helping think of justifications for its

actions? If so, are there any other kinds of cases—such as breach of contract, negligence, or employment discrimination—where it is appropriate for judges to help the government win by inventing justifications for its actions?

- If you had to "negative" every conceivable objection to your being a judge in order to be confirmed, do you think that would be a fair standard? Do you think it would be fair for senators to vote against your nomination on the basis of purely speculative concerns for which no evidence has been offered?

- Deciding constitutional cases is a difficult undertaking in which there is often no clear answer. As a judge, would you err on the side of individual liberty or government power?

A final point to make is that no one should be disqualified from serving as a judge just for having strong feelings about the Constitution. For too long, the strategy for choosing nominees and getting them through the confirmation process has been to look for people who are smart and capable but who either do not have strong feelings about constitutional law or have mostly kept whatever feelings they do have to themselves. That should change. Populating our courts with judges who see no major problems with the status quo is a recipe for more of the same. Think how much different things would be if government had to justify its actions to us instead of the other way around. It's not too much to ask for—we just need courts to be consistent about requiring it.

KEEPING *ROE* IN PERSPECTIVE

In arguing for a more engaged judiciary, one inevitably encounters the gravitational pull of *Roe v. Wade*.[4] Indeed, the abortion issue may be likened to a jurisprudential black hole, bending the light of reason and warping the surrounding constitutional space. And while I cannot prove it, I suspect that much of the antipathy in certain quarters toward unenumerated rights flows not from a general hostility to liberty or a strong faith in the efficacy, wisdom, or justice of government, but from a desire to deny any purchase to arguments in favor of a constitutionally protected right to abortion. That sentiment is certainly understandable for people who believe that human life begins at conception, but I think it is misguided nevertheless.

Although it is impossible to resolve the constitutional status of abortion to everyone's satisfaction, the quality of the debate could certainly benefit from greater clarity and consistency. This includes, first, discarding the argument that there is no right to abortion just because the Constitution does not specifically mention one. The Constitution is most plausibly read to acknowledge the existence of unenumerated rights, and for more than a century the Supreme Court has consistently held that it protects at least some rights not expressly mentioned in the text. That conclusion has not been controversial among the general public.

Two of the earliest and best-known cases protecting unenumerated rights are *Meyer v. Nebraska* (1923)[5] and *Pierce v. Society of Sisters* (1925).[6] Both cases involved the ability of parents to guide the upbringing and education of their children. The law at issue in *Meyer* prohibited teaching foreign languages to children before they had completed eighth grade. In *Pierce*, the question was whether Oregon could outlaw private schools and require all parents to send their children to public schools. The Supreme Court found that both laws violated the Fourteenth Amendment under the theory, discussed above, that has come to be called "substantive due process." Neither opinion contains significant historical or legal analysis; both essentially rest instead on the bald assertion that "the individual has certain fundamental rights which must be respected."[7] Though not specifically spelled out in the text of the Constitution, these rights include "the liberty of parents and guardians to direct the upbringing and education of children under their control."[8] Perhaps recognizing that he is making little more than a bare assertion here, Justice McReynolds contrasts his vision of America with Plato's suggestion that children be raised by the state and that "'no parent is to know his own child, nor any child his parent.'"[9]

That image is no doubt deeply disturbing to most Americans, and yet so-called "strict constructionists" apparently see no constitutional impediment to that arrangement because they categorically reject the legitimacy of judges protecting unenumerated rights. (I say "so-called" because a more accurate term for many of them would be *"selective strict constructionists,"* as exemplified by Judge Robert Bork's refusal to give any substance to the Ninth Amendment or the Fourteenth Amendment's privileges or immunities clause.)[10] Although its jurisprudential foundation may be thin, the unenumerated constitutional right of parents to guide the upbringing of their children has remained utterly uncontroversial for nearly a century. The same goes for other unenumerated rights of more recent vintage, including the rights to marry,[11] travel,[12] live with members of one's extended family,[13] and not be sterilized for eugenic purposes.[14]

Yet another unenumerated right that has been uncontroversial in principle (though applying it to specific situations presents challenges, as with all constitutional rights) is the ability to defend oneself from violence or other sudden danger. The Supreme Court described this right as a "central component" of the Second Amendment in *District of Columbia v. Heller,* and the majority sharply rejected Justice Breyer's "assertion that individual self-defense is merely a 'subsidiary interest' of the right to keep and bear arms."[15] Lower courts have held that the constitutional right of self-preservation includes not having the government cut off potential means of rescue when a person's life is in danger, as happened in one tragic case where a twelve-year-old boy fell into Lake Michigan and a deputy sheriff, enforcing county policy, threatened to arrest anyone who tried to rescue him, including a pair of scuba divers who happened to be on the scene with their own boat. It took the government-approved rescuers thirty minutes to pull the boy out of the water, by which time he had drowned.[16]

Of course, the issue of self-preservation can arise in the context of pregnancies as well, and even the dissenting justices in *Roe v. Wade* suggested that a law prohibiting abortions "where the mother's life is in jeopardy" would be constitutionally suspect.[17] Assuming it is legitimate for courts to protect some unenumerated constitutional rights—which it appears few people dispute, at least when confronted with the full implications of that position—and assuming further that self-defense and self-preservation are among those rights, then it seems unlikely the Supreme Court will withdraw from the abortion issue completely, even if its role were limited to determining the scope of the medical necessity exemption.

To be sure, there are strong arguments against finding a broader constitutional right to abortion. But the strength of those arguments does not lie in the premise that there is no constitutional basis for protecting *any* unenumerated rights, as Judge Bork and others have claimed.[18] Instead, it lies mainly in the government's obligation to protect equally the rights of all persons, including persons who have not yet been born. Determining when personhood begins is not something that judges are uniquely equipped to do, though there may be some role for them in ensuring that legislatures do not exercise that power arbitrarily or invidiously.

It is simply not true, however, that anyone who supports judicial protection for unenumerated constitutional rights like occupational freedom must, to be consistent, support a right to non-medically-necessary abortions as well. Judge Bork expressed that view in *The Tempting of America* by asserting that *"Dred Scott, Lochner,* and *Roe* are equally valid examples of constitutional law" once one accepts the legitimacy of courts enforcing unenumerated rights through substantive due process.[19] More recently, a prominent progressive scholar has seized on that maxim—the idea that *Lochner*'s protection of economic liberty is indistinguishable from *Roe*'s protection of abortion—as a kind of talisman to discourage conservatives from reconsidering the current policy of judicial abdication with respect to economic liberties.[20] But they are wrong that *Lochner* necessarily entails *Roe*. The textual and historical arguments in favor of occupational freedom are compelling, and protecting economic liberty appears to have been among the chief concerns of those who framed and ratified the Fourteenth Amendment. To be sure, it protects other rights as well, but the notion that the arguments for the right to earn a living and the right to have an abortion are coextensive and indistinguishable is utterly baseless.

REALITY CHECK

In order to fully embrace judicial engagement, it is necessary to reject three pervasive myths: first, that *preventing* people from enforcing laws amounts to "judicial tyranny"; second, that judicial review is an all-or-nothing proposition whereby striking down a given law necessarily removes that whole issue from the political process; and third, that there are other ways to achieve constitutionally limited government than with a properly engaged judiciary. These myths may have a seductive appeal to some, but they are wrong nevertheless.

In his recent book calling for a renewed commitment to judicial deference, Judge J. Harvie Wilkinson speaks often of what he calls the "inalienable right of self-governance." For example, he argues that "[t]he great casualty of cosmic constitutional theory"—by which he appears to mean *any* constitutional theory—has been our "inalienable right of self-governance."[21] He repeats this lament near the end of the book, where he argues that "[t]he grand quest of the theorists has left [judicial] restraint by the wayside and placed the inalienable right of Americans to self-governance at unprecedented risk."[22] But Judge Wilkinson never explains precisely what he means by the "right of self-governance," and it becomes clear in reading his book that what he is really talking about is not the ability of individuals to control their own lives, but rather their ability to control *other people's* lives through the coercive power of law.

In this, Judge Wilkinson's argument appears quite similar to the one Justice Stephen Breyer makes in his widely read book *Active Liberty*. Breyer identifies two different kinds of liberty, which he calls the "liberty of the ancients" and the "liberty of the moderns."[23] But as with "self-governance" in Judge Wilkinson's book, it becomes clear that one of those terms is euphemistic. The liberty of the ancients—or "active liberty," as Justice Breyer calls it—is the right to participate in government; it is the "sharing of a nation's sovereign authority among its people."[24] But this begs the question of what the sovereign authority of a nation or state encompasses. Does it include the authority to sterilize the "socially inadequate," as the Supreme Court infamously held in *Buck v. Bell*,[25] or the ability to "dish[] out special economic benefits" to favored individuals or industries by enforcing nakedly anticompetitive licensing laws, like the State of Oklahoma continues to do by permitting only state-licensed funeral directors to sell caskets?[26] And how willing should courts be to accept at face value a legislature's assertion that it is actually exercising its "sovereign authority" when history, experience, and public choice theory show that often it will merely be pretending to do so while pursuing constitutionally forbidden ends?

These questions matter because there is no inherent right to impose our will on other people just because we outnumber them. There is no such thing as an "inalienable right of self-governance" where "self-governance" really means the ability of political majorities to exercise arbitrary power over others. Any time you seek to bend another person to your will, you owe that person a reasoned explanation. That is a basic moral duty, and it cannot be relieved by any political system, even a democracy. Judicial review—or, more precisely, judicial engagement—is the process by which we ensure that every person receives the reasoned explanation to which they are entitled before they are required to obey a law they may not agree with. Refusing to play a serious role in that process is not judicial modesty, it is abdication.

The second myth to be rejected is the notion that in declaring a particular law unconstitutional, courts necessarily remove that entire subject matter from the realm of public policy. Judge Wilkinson, for example, argues that "the club of unconstitutionality [should be] a weapon of last resort, precisely because it so often knocks every other player out of the ring."[27] Other proponents of extreme judicial restraint make that assertion as well, but their concerns are overstated.[28] The reality is that judges can adjust the scope of their rulings to reflect their level of confidence in their interpretation of the Constitution, or to minimize the disruptive effect of those rulings when appropriate.

For example, the Supreme Court has never explicitly overruled its decision in *Buck v. Bell* (1927) upholding the constitutionality of compulsory sterilization,[29] though its ruling in *Skinner v. Oklahoma* (1942),[30] rejecting sterilization as punishment for certain crimes of moral turpitude, is commonly understood as an indication that the Court would certainly do so were the question presented to it again. Given what has transpired since 1927, including the horror of Nazi eugenics, a modern judge might well feel sufficiently confident about the existence of an unenumerated right against involuntary steriliza-tion to write a broad decision taking eugenic sterilization completely off the table. By contrast, a judge who felt less confident about the existence or scope of a particular right could rule more narrowly—holding, for example, that while the Constitution does not prevent government from regulating experimental cancer drugs across the board, the government must nevertheless present some evidence that a particular patient is likely to be made worse off by taking a certain drug than not taking it.

For a further illustration, consider the Institute for Justice's chal-lenges to laws regulating African hair braiders. African hair braiding is a natural hairstyling technique that dates back many centuries and involves weaving and locking hair into cornrows and other patterns that are both artistic and functional. Many states require hair braiders to be fully licensed cosmetologists, even when they provide no other services and use no scissors, chemicals, or potentially hazardous instru-ments. There is virtually no overlap between the knowledge and skills that hair braiders use in their work and the knowledge and skills they must master in order to get a cosmetology license.[31] And the amount

of training required (even if it were relevant) is often utterly disproportionate to any conceivable risks posed by hair braiding. In Utah,
for example, the licensing process included two thousand hours of
government-mandated cosmetology training, which is enough time
to qualify as an armed security guard, a mortgage loan originator,
a real estate sales agent, an emergency medical technician, and a
lawyer—combined![32]

The Institute for Justice has challenged licensing requirements
for hair braiders in court and has prevailed in two out of three cases,
including Utah most recently.[33] Contrary to the fears expressed by
proponents of judicial restraint, neither of the two winning decisions
presumed to take licensing for hair braiders completely off the table;
instead, they simply held that, on the record presented, the government
had not shown an adequate fit between its stated public welfare concerns and the arbitrary and sweeping means it had chosen to address
those concerns. Nothing in these decisions prevents the government
from trying again with a more carefully tailored law. Whether new
laws will be enacted and whether any such laws will pass constitutional
muster remain to be seen. Perhaps it will turn out that the menace of
unlicensed hair braiding isn't that big a deal to legislatures after all.

The final myth to be overcome is that there is some way to have
constitutionally limited government besides judicial engagement.
Believing our system will work without a properly engaged judiciary is
like believing that an engine will run without a carburetor—it wasn't
designed to work that way, and it won't work that way. It is simply no
use hoping that future generations of politicians will see the abuses
inherent in lobbying, logrolling, and interest-group capture of regulatory agencies, and suddenly decide to rein themselves in voluntarily.
With trillions of dollars in play every year and constituents who expect
a steady supply of pork from Washington, there is no realistic prospect of the system reforming itself from the inside. Nor is it a matter
of "throwing the bums out." The vast majority of public officials are
decent, patriotic people who take seriously their duty to act in the

public good. But the incentives to exercise forbidden powers and cater to interest groups are simply too strong.

Another idea currently in vogue is to amend the Constitution in order to address some of the problems with overweening government discussed in this book. But why should we suppose that courts will be any more inclined to enforce new restrictions on government than they have been to enforce existing ones? When the Supreme Court rewrites laws in order to uphold them, as it did with Obamacare, that problem cannot be solved with a constitutional amendment. When courts are prepared to interpret constitutional provisions like the contract clause or the public-use requirement of the Fifth Amendment as allowing the precise abuses they were designed to forbid, nothing will stop them from doing so with new restrictions. And when courts relieve the government of the obligation to justify its actions with honest explanations and admissible evidence, the problem lies not with the Constitution but with the judiciary.

Our nation was conceived in liberty, and the promise of constitutionally limited government is every American's birthright. We have strayed from those ideals, but not so far that we cannot recover them. Judicial engagement is how we can do it.

Acknowledgments

I am indebted to all of my colleagues at the Institute for Justice, whose commitment to liberty is a constant source of inspiration. IJ president and general counsel Chip Mellor coined the term "judicial engagement," proposed this book, and provided just the right mix of encouragement and boot leather to make sure it got done. I am grateful to Steve Simpson for helping light the way through many hours of discussion and debate; to my research assistant Laura Lieberman for constantly surpassing my expectations; to Bob McNamara and Paul Sherman for their innumerable contributions and boundless patience; to Lisa Knepper for insisting on "more Constitution"; to Dana Berliner, Jeff Rowes, Bob Levy, and Will Baude for their reviews and suggestions; and to John Kramer, Shira Rawlinson, and the rest of IJ's stellar communications team for their tireless efforts to spread the word about judicial engagement. Thanks also to Professor Randy Barnett for showing why the Constitution is, first and foremost, a charter of liberty.

This book would not have happened without the enthusiastic support of Roger Kimball, publisher of Encounter Books, and the hard work and consummate professionalism of my editor, Carol Staswick.

To Judge Royce Lamberth, for whom I had the honor of serving as a law clerk, and his wife Janice—thank you for everything. I would also like to thank my family and especially my wife Nicki for their love and support.

Finally, to IJ's clients. It takes guts to stand up for freedom and real dedication to stay the course. You are my heroes.

Notes

Introduction

1. The term "judicial engagement" was coined by the Institute for Justice's president and general counsel, Chip Mellor, in a 2005 article he wrote for the Institute's newsletter *Law & Liberty* titled "Judicial Activism and Judicial Restraint: Two Paths to Bigger Government," available at http://www.ij.org/two-paths-to-bigger-government-2.

2. 1 *Annals of Cong.* 457 (Joseph Gales ed., 1834).

3. Susan Page, "Poll: Romney Preferred Over Obama to Handle the Economy," *USA Today*, July 23, 2012, http://usatoday30.usatoday.com/news/politics/story/2012-07-23/poll-romney-obama-economy/56439758/1 (reporting results of a July 2012 *USA Today* / Gallup poll that showed 61 percent of Americans are frustrated with the expansion of government power); see also "CNN Poll: Big Shifts on Role of Government," CNN, October 3, 2012, http://politicalticker.blogs.cnn.com/2012/10/03/cnn-poll-big-shifts-on-role-of-government/ (reporting results of CNN / ORC International poll showing that 6 in 10 Americans "say the government is doing too much that should be left to individuals"). Additionally, a Pew Research poll conducted in January 2013 found that a majority of Americans believe that the federal government has too much power over individual rights. "Majority Says the Federal Government Threatens Their Personal Rights," Pew Research Center for the People

and the Press, January 31, 2013, http://www.people-press.org/2013/01/31/
majority-says-the-federal-government-threatens-their-personal-rights/.

4. See, e.g., Robert A. Levy & William Mellor, *The Dirty Dozen: How Twelve
Supreme Court Cases Radically Expanded Government and Eroded Freedom* (2008).

5. *Cooksey v. Futrell*, No. 12-2084, 2013 WL 3215240 (4th Cir. June 27,
2013). Information about the case is available at http://ij.org/paleospeech.

6. *Bokhari v. Nashville*, No. 3:11-00088 (M.D. Tenn. filed Apr. 20, 2011).
Information about the case is available at http://ij.org/nashville-limos.

7. *Worley v. Florida Secretary of State*, 717 F.3d 1238 (11th Cir. 2013). Information about the case is available at http://ij.org/florida-citizen-speech.

8. See, e.g., Harvey Silverglate, *Three Felonies a Day: How the Feds Target the
Innocent* (2009); Alex Kozinski & Misha Tseytlin, "You're (Probably) a Federal
Criminal," in *In the Name of Justice: Leading Experts Reexamine the Classic Article
"The Aims of the Criminal Law"* 43, 44–49 (Timothy Lynch ed., 2009); Gene
Healy, *Go Directly to Jail: The Criminalization of Almost Everything* (2004); Glenn
Harlan Reynolds, "Ham Sandwich Nation: Due Process When Everything
is a Crime," University of Tennessee Legal Studies Research Paper No. 206
(2013), available at http://ssrn.com/abstract=2203713.

9. "The Joy of Tax: A Futile Plea for Simplicity," *Economist*, April 8, 2010,
http://www.economist.com/node/15867984?story_id=15867984.

10. Elizabeth Flock, "President Obama Has Outspent Last Five Presi-
dents," *U.S. News & World Report*, June 1, 2012, http://www.usnews.
com/news/blogs/washington-whispers/2012/06/01/president-obama-
has-outspent-last-five-presidents.

11. "U.S. Currency FAQs," Bureau of Engraving & Printing, http://www.
moneyfactory.gov/faqlibrary.html (reporting the weight of a bill, "regardless of denomination," as approximately 1 gram); "Blue Whale," *National
Geographic*, http://animals.nationalgeographic.com/animals/mammals/
blue-whale/ (noting that blue whales can weigh up to 200 tons (181,437 kg)).

12. These numbers are all approximate, in part because it is impossible to
be precise with figures of this magnitude. The calculations are based on a
slightly optimistic annual federal revenue of $2.5 trillion. Dividing the $16
trillion federal debt by $2.5 trillion annual revenue produces a multiplier of

6.4. The median family income of $50,000 multiplied by 6.4 equals $320,000. Dividing federal debt and unfunded obligations of $80 trillion by $2.5 trillion annual revenue produces a multiplier of 32. Multiplying 32 by the median income of $50,000 equals $1.6 million.

13. *907 Whitehead St. Inc., v. Sec'y of Agric.*, 701 F.3d 1345, 1351 (11th Cir. 2012).

14. U.S. Const. amend. VI.

15. U.S. Const. amend. V.

16. U.S. Const. amend. I.

17. U.S. Const. amends. XV & XIX.

18. U.S. Const. amend. II. See also *District of Columbia v. Heller*, 554 U.S. 570 (2008) and *McDonald v. City of Chicago*, 130 S. Ct. 3020 (2010) (striking down Washington D.C.'s and Chicago's handgun bans, respectively).

19. U.S. Const. amends. VI & VII.

20. U.S. Const. amend. I.

Chapter 1: Constitutional Law for Ordinary People

1. Katie Lannan, "Tewksbury Motel Feels Fed Heat, but More Drug Arrests Nearby," *Lowell Sun*, January 13, 2013, available at http://www.lowellsun.com/photocontest/ci_22365659/tewksbury-motel-feels-fed-heat-but-more-drug.

2. *United States v. 434 Main Street, Tewksbury, Mass.*, No. 0911635JGD, 2013 U.S. Dist. LEXIS 9730, at *81 (D. Mass. Jan. 24, 2103), available at http://ij.org/images/pdf_folder/private_property/forfeiture/caswellopinion-1-24-13.pdf. The government chose not to appeal Judge Dein's ruling.

3. Marian R. Williams et al., Institute for Justice, *Policing for Profit: The Abuse of Civil Asset Forfeiture* (2010), available at http://www.ij.org/images/pdf_folder/other_pubs/assetforfeituretoemail.pdf (examining each state's civil forfeiture laws and the benefits that state governments receive through those seizures of private property).

4. *United States v. $35,131.00 in United States Currency*, No. Action H112659, slip op. at 3 (S.D. Tex. Apr. 2, 2012), available at http://www.volokh.com/wp-content/uploads/2012/04/35131.pdf.

5. *Kelo v. City of New London*, 545 U.S. 469 (2005) (authorizing eminent domain for economic development); *Armour v. City of Indianapolis*, 132 S. Ct. 2073 (2012) (upholding grossly disproportionate charges for municipal sewer hookups); *Nebbia v. New York*, 291 U.S. 502 (1934) (upholding a New York law setting minimum prices for milk).

6. *Kelo v. City of New London* at 518 (Thomas, J., dissenting).

7. *Nat'l Fed'n of Indep. Bus. v. Sebelius*, 132 S. Ct. 2566, 2577 (2012) (emphasis added).

8. U.S. Const. amend. X.

9. *Clemens v. Maryland State Bd. of Veterinary Med. Exam'rs*, No. 29766V, slip op. at 2 (Montgomery Cnty. Cir. Ct. Aug. 11, 2009). Copy on file with the Institute for Justice.

10. *Cruz v. Town of Cicero*, 275 F.3d 579 (7th Cir. 2001).

11. *Id.* at 588.

12. *Nollan v. California Coastal Comm'n*, 483 U.S. 825, 834 (1987).

13. Randy E. Barnett, *Restoring the Lost Constitution: The Presumption of Liberty* 319 (2004).

14. See also Kermit Roosevelt III, *The Myth of Judicial Activism: Making Sense of Supreme Court Decisions* 120–23 (2006) (explaining that due process requires government to "act in the public interest"); David E. Bernstein, *Rehabilitating Lochner: Defending Individual Rights against Progressive Reform* 11–14 (2011) (discussing Supreme Court cases recognizing that "'there are limitations on [government] power which grow out of the essential nature of all free governments'") (quoting *Loan Ass'n v. Topeka*, 87 U.S. (20 Wall.) 655, 663 (1875)).

For a particularly thorough discussion of how the Fourteenth Amendment's due process clause prohibits states from depriving people of life, liberty, or property "except for good reason," see Timothy Sandefur, "In Defense of Substantive Due Process, or the Promise of Lawful Rule," 35 *Harv. J.L. & Pub. Pol'y* 284, 285 (2012). Sandefur also explains why "it is not in principle possible for courts to avoid addressing the question of whether a challenged law advances a legitimate government interest—or deciding which government interests are or are not 'legitimate.'" *Id.* at 23.

15. U.S. Const. art. 1, § 9, cl. 2; *id.* art. 1, § 10, cl. 1; *id.* amend. I; *id.* amend. II; *id.* amend. VIII.

16. In fact, the question of whether some rights were so "trivial" or obvious that it would be pointless to include them in the Constitution provoked significant disagreement during the ratification debates. The right to wear a hat is an example of a trivial (but potentially symbolically important) right that actually arose during debates, and the right to hunt and to fish on one's own land were examples of rights so obvious (at the time) that many thought they did not bear mentioning. See, e.g., Philip A. Hamburger, "Trivial Rights," 70 *Notre Dame L. Rev.* 1 (1994).

17. 1 *Annals of Cong.* 759–60 (Joseph Gales ed., 1834), quoted in Randy E. Barnett, *Restoring the Lost Constitution: The Presumption of Liberty* 58 (2004).

18. 4 *The Debates in the Several State Conventions on the Adoption of the Federal Constitution as Recommended by the General Convention at Philadelphia in 1787*, at 167 (J. Elliot ed., 2d ed. 1836) (Remarks of James Iredell in the North Carolina Convention, July 29, 1788), quoted in Barnett, *Restoring the Lost Constitution* at 57.

19. 32 U.S. 243 (1833).

20. For a detailed discussion of the historical basis for substantive due process see Frederick M. Geddicks, "An Originalist Defense of Substantive Due Process: Magna Carta, Higher Law, Constitutionalism, and the Fifth Amendment," 58 *Emory L.J.* 585 (2009) and Timothy Sandefur, "In Defense of Substantive Due Process, or the Promise of Lawful Rule," 35 *Harv. J.L. & Pub. Pol'y* 284, 284–93 (2012). See also Barnett, *Restoring the Lost Constitution* at 207.

Notable critics of substantive due process include Judge Robert Bork, Professor Raoul Berger, and Professor Lino Graglia, who argue that the due process clause is limited to issues of procedural fairness. They also believe that substantive due process serves as a vehicle for judges to project their own personal preferences onto the Constitution. Berger disparages this as "government by judiciary." See Raoul Berger, *Government by Judiciary: The Transformation of the Fourteenth Amendment* 273 (Liberty Fund 2d ed. 1997) (1977). Graglia considers substantive due process an "oxymoron[]" that allows the

Court to reserve particular policy issues "for final decision." Lino A. Graglia, "Originalism and the Constitution: Does Originalism Always Provide the Answer?" 34 *Harv. J.L. & Pub. Pol'y* 73, 77 (2011). And Judge Bork argues that substantive due process "has been used countless times by judges who want to write their personal beliefs into a document that, most inconveniently, does not contain those beliefs." Robert H. Bork, *The Tempting of America: The Political Seduction of the Law* 31 (1990).

21. 274 U.S. 200 (1927).

22. *Buck v. Bell*, 274 U.S. 200, 205 (1927). It appears from subsequent scholarship that none of those things was true. Carrie Buck was a woman of average intelligence, and her daughter appears also to have been of average intelligence. See, e.g., Stephen Jay Gould, "Carrie Buck's Daughter," *Natural History*, July 1984, at 14, available at http://archive.org/stream/naturalhistory93unse#page/n691/mode/2up/search/Carrie+Buck. Gould explains that Carrie Buck, one of her mother's many illegitimate children, came from an impoverished, uncouth background. After being raped by a member of her adoptive family, she was committed to an institution to "hide her shame (and her rapist's identity)." *Id.* at 17. She was also blamed for getting pregnant. Gould's article notes that her daughter Vivian received average grades on her report card and even made the honor roll at one point before her early death. *Id.* at 18. Gould states that Carrie Buck's case "never was about mental deficiency; it was always a matter of sexual morality and social deviance." *Id.* at 17.

23. *Buck v. Bell* at 207 (internal citation omitted).

24. 106 U.S. 583 (1883).

25. 388 U.S. 1 (1967).

26. *Pierce v. Soc'y of Sisters*, 268 U.S. 510 (1925); *Meyer v. Nebraska*, 262 U.S. 390 (1923).

27. *Meyer v. Nebraska* at 399.

28. *United States v. Jones*, 132 S. Ct. 945 (2012).

29. President George W. Bush, for example, was properly criticized for signing the Bipartisan Campaign Reform Act of 2002, also known as "McCain-Feingold," despite "reservations about the constitutionality of the

broad ban on issue advertising." White House Press Release, "President Signs Campaign Finance Reform Act," March 27, 2002, available at http://georgewbush-whitehouse.archives.gov/news/releases/2002/03/20020327.html. Among other critics, the editors of *National Review* branded the act as a dangerous threat to free speech and "one of the worst moments of George W. Bush's presidency." "A Clear Danger to Free Speech," *National Review Online*, March 27, 2009, http://www.nationalreview.com/articles/227175/clear-danger-free-speech/editors.

30. See, e.g., Suzanna Sherry, "Why We Need More Judicial Activism" (forthcoming in *Constitutionalism, Executive Power, and Popular Enlightenment*, 2014), Vanderbilt Public Law Research Paper No. 133 (February 6, 2013), available at http://ssrn.com/abstract=2213372. As Professor Sherry explains, "Judicial review, despite some claims to the contrary, is not judicial supremacy. Courts are the final arbiter of the Constitution only to the extent that they hold a law *un*constitutional, and even then only because they act last in time, not because their will is supreme." *Id.* at 2.

31. James Madison explained in *Federalist* 10:

> No man is allowed to be the judge in his own cause, because his interest would certainly bias his own judgment, and, not improbably, corrupt his integrity. With equal, nay with greater reason, a body of men are unfit to be both judges and parties at the same time; yet what are many of the most important acts of legislation but many judicial determinations, not indeed concerning the rights of single persons, but concerning the rights of large bodies of citizens? And what are the different classes of legislators but advocates and parties to the causes which they determine?

The Federalist No. 10, at 79 (James Madison) (Clinton Rossiter ed., 1961). See also *Lopez v. Thurmer*, 573 F.3d 484, 492–93 (7th Cir. 2009) ("In essence, the Court of Appeals of Wisconsin allowed the Sheriff's Department to judge its own case. The constitutional infirmity of such a methodology is, to put it mildly, firmly established.")

32. Barnett, *Restoring the Lost Constitution* at 11–52.

33. Mark R. Levin, *Men in Black: How the Supreme Court Is Destroying America* 33 (2005).

34. *Id.* at 23–33.

35. *Id.* at 16 (arguing that the Supreme Court's opinion in *Korematsu v. United States* was "devoid of any legitimate constitutional basis for upholding Roosevelt's" internment policy); *id.* at 143–57 (claiming that the Supreme Court's failure to strike down campaign finance laws amounts to "silencing political debate"); *id.* at 131–41 (asserting that failing to strike down expansive federal laws amounts to "socialism from the bench"); *id.* at 89–99 (equating affirmative action with "endorsing racism").

36. *Id.* at 131 (federalism), 89 (affirmative action), 143 (campaign finance).

37. 323 U.S. 214 (1944).

38. 545 U.S. 469 (2005).

Chapter 2: How Courts Protect Rights They Care About

1. For a detailed discussion of the Supreme Court's tendency to divide rights into those that get significant judicial review and those that do not, see Jeffrey D. Jackson, "Putting Rationality Back into the Rational Basis Test: Saving Substantive Due Process and Redeeming the Promise of the Ninth Amendment," 45 *U. Rich. L. Rev.* 491 (2011). Professor Jackson explains that the Court's current version of tiered scrutiny "forces courts to face the prospect of classifying a right as fundamental, and thus taking it outside the arena of public debate and legislative action, or applying a rational basis standard akin to no review at all." *Id.* at 547–48.

2. *Washington v. Glucksberg*, 521 U.S. 702, 720–21 (1997) (internal quotations and citation omitted).

3. See, e.g., *Zablocki v. Redhail*, 434 U.S. 374 (1978) (right to marry); *Loving v. Virginia*, 388 U.S. 1 (1967) (interracial marriage); *Carey v. Population Servs. Int'l*, 431 U.S. 678 (1977) (contraception); *Eisenstadt v. Baird*, 405 U.S. 438 (1972) (same); *Troxel v. Granville*, 530 U.S. 57 (2000) (rearing one's own children); *Shapiro v. Thompson*, 394 U.S. 618 (1969) (travel); *Crandall v. Nevada*, 73 U.S. 35 (1868) (travel).

4. See Marc Schlueb, "Couple Clash with Orlando City Hall over Vegetable Garden," *Orlando Sentinel*, January 9, 2013, http://articles.orlandosentinel. com/2013-01-09/news/os-gardens-prohibited-in-orlando-20130109_1_small-garden-front-yard-vegetable (describing Orlando couple's effort to keep their front-yard vegetable garden after being cited for violating city ordinance requiring "traditional landscaping" for front yards); Rick Barrett, "Dairy Farmer Vernon Hershberger Receives $1,000 Fine in Raw Milk Case," *Milwaukee Journal Sentinel*, June 13, 2013, http://www.jsonline.com/business/dairy-farmer-vernon-hershberger-to-be-sentenced-in-raw-milk-case-b9933112z1-211383841.html (describing state's unsuccessful effort to prosecute a Wisconsin farmer for selling raw milk).

5. *Abigail Alliance for Better Access to Developmental Drugs v. Eschenbach*, 495 F.3d 695 (D.C. Cir. 2007) (en banc) (terminally ill cancer patients have no fundamental right of access to potentially life-saving experimental cancer drugs); *City of New Orleans v. Dukes*, 427 U.S. 297 (1976) (no fundamental right to earn a living in the occupation of one's choice); *Village of Belle Terre v. Boraas*, 416 U.S. 1 (1974) (no fundamental right for unrelated persons to live together in the same house).

6. *Church of the Lukumi Babalu Aye, Inc. v. City of Hialeah*, 508 U.S. 520, 534–35 (1993).

7. David B. Rivkin Jr. & Andrew M. Grossman, "Gun Control and the Constitution," *Wall Street Journal*, February 11, 2013, at A13, available at http://online.wsj.com/article/SB10001424127887323951904578290460073953432.html.

8. *Maryland v. King*, 133 S. Ct. 1958, 1980 (2013) (Scalia, J., dissenting).

9. Transcript of Oral Argument at 47–48, *Ariz. Free Enter. Club's Freedom Club PAC v. Bennett*, 131 S. Ct. 2806 (2011) (No. 10-328), available at http://www.supremecourt.gov/oral_arguments/argument_transcripts/10-238.pdf.

10. See, e.g., *Pagan v. Fruchey*, 492 F.3d 766, 770–71 (6th Cir. 2007) (en banc) (citing *Cent. Hudson Gas & Elec. Corp. v. Pub. Serv. Comm'n of N.Y.*, 447 U.S. 557, 563–64 (1980) and *Fla. Bar v. Went For It, Inc.*, 515 U.S. 618, 624 (1995)).

11. *Pagan v. Fruchey* at 771 (quoting *Fla. Bar v. Went For It, Inc.* at 626).

12. *Id.* at 773 (quoting the affidavit of Police Chief Matt Fruchey).

13. *Id.* at 775.

14. *Byrum v. Landreth*, 566 F.3d 442, 449 (5th Cir. 2009).

15. The interior design industry has been a hotbed of anticompetitive lob-
bying efforts, led by a group called the American Society of Interior Designers.
These efforts are documented in a series of studies commissioned by the
Institute for Justice. See Dick M. Carpenter II, Institute for Justice, *Designing
Cartels: How Industry Insiders Cut Out Competition* (2007); Dick M. Carpenter II,
Institute for Justice, *Designed to Mislead: How Industry Insiders Mislead the Public
About the Need for Interior Design Regulation* (2008); and David E. Harrington &
Jaret Traber, Institute for Justice, *Designed to Exclude: How Interior Design Insiders
Use Government Power to Exclude Minorities and Burden Consumers* (2009); all avail-
able at http://www.ij.org/interior-design-litigation-summary.

16. See *Dent v. West Virginia*, 129 U.S. 114, 121 (1889) ("It is undoubtedly
the right of every citizen of the United States to follow any lawful calling,
business, or profession he may choose, subject only to such restrictions as are
imposed upon all persons of like age, sex, and condition."); *Allgeyer v. Louisiana*,
165 U.S. 578, 589 (1897) (recognizing the right "to pursue any livelihood or
avocation"); *Truax v. Raich*, 239 U.S. 33, 41 (1915) (holding that "the right to
work for a living in the common occupations of the community is of the very
essence of the personal freedom and opportunity that it was the purpose of
the Amendment to secure"); *Meyer v. Nebraska*, 262 U.S. 390, 399–400 (1923)
(the Fourteenth Amendment's conception of "liberty" includes the right "to
engage in any of the common occupations of life"); *New State Ice Co. v. Lieb-
mann*, 285 U.S. 262, 278 (1932) ("[N]othing is more clearly settled than that
it is beyond the power of a state, under the guise of protecting the public,
arbitrarily to interfere with private business or prohibit lawful occupations
or impose unreasonable and unnecessary restrictions upon them.") (internal
quotations and citations omitted); *Schware v. Bd. of Bar Exam'rs*, 353 U.S. 232,
238–39 (1957) ("A State cannot exclude a person from the practice of law or
from any other occupation in a manner or for reasons that contravene the
Due Process or Equal Protection Clause of the Fourteenth Amendment."); *Bd.
of Regents v. Roth*, 408 U.S. 564, 572 (1972) (recognizing the right "to engage
in any of the common occupations of life"); *New Hampshire v. Piper*, 470 U.S.

274, 280 n.9 (1985) (noting that the Court has recognized that "the pursuit of a common calling is one of the most fundamental of those privileges protected" by the privileges and immunities clause of Article IV—not to be confused with the Fourteenth Amendment's privileges or immunities clause, which the Court has essentially deleted from the Constitution); *Lowe v. SEC*, 472 U.S. 181, 228 (1985) (noting that citizens have a right to follow any lawful calling subject to licensing requirements that are rationally related to their "fitness or capacity to practice the profession") (internal quotation and citation omitted); *Connecticut v. Gabbert*, 526 U.S. 286, 291–92 (1999) ("This Court has indicated that the liberty component of the Fourteenth Amendment's Due Process Clause includes some generalized due process right to choose one's field of private employment, but a right which is nevertheless subject to reasonable government regulation."). See also *Barsky v. Bd. of Regents*, 347 U.S. 442, 472–73 (1945) (Douglas, J., dissenting) ("The right to work, I had assumed, was the most precious liberty that man possesses.").

17. See, e.g., Timothy Sandefur, *The Right to Earn a Living: Economic Freedom and the Law* 18–23 (2010) (describing legal challenges to trade monopolies in England in the seventeenth and eighteenth centuries).

18. *Yick Wo v. Hopkins*, 118 U.S. 366–67 (1886).

19. *Id.* at 366 (emphasis added).

20. *Id.* at 374.

21. *In re Jacobs*, 98 N.Y. 98 (N.Y. 1885).

22. *Id.* at 115.

23. *Id.* at 104.

24. *Id.* at 114.

25. David E. Bernstein, *Rehabilitating Lochner: Defending Individual Rights against Progressive Reform* 138 n.85 (2011).

26. *In re Jacobs* at 114–15.

27. 1 *Annals of Cong.* 457 (Joseph Gales ed., 1834).

28. 198 U.S. 45 (1905).

29. Bernstein, *Rehabilitating Lochner* at 24 (quoting "Now for the Ten-Hour Day," *Baker's Journal*, April 20, 1895, at 1).

30. *Id.*

31. *Id.* at 27.

32. *Id.* at 31.

33. The fascinating story of the *Lochner* case is told in much greater detail in Chapter 2 of Professor Bernstein's *Rehabilitating Lochner*.

34. See *Lochner v. New York*, 198 U.S. 45, 55–58 (1905) (citing *Jacobson v. Massachusetts*, 197 U.S. 11 (1905) and *Knoxville Iron Co. v. Harbison*, 183 U.S. 13 (1901)).

35. *Id.* at 64.

36. *Id.*

37. *Id.* at 56–57.

38. *Id.* at 65 (Harlan, J., dissenting) (internal quotation omitted).

39. *Id.* at 66, 68 (Harlan, J., dissenting) (emphasis added).

40. *Id.* at 68 (Harlan, J., dissenting).

41. *Id.* at 70 (Harlan, J., dissenting).

42. *Id.* at 75 (Holmes, J., dissenting).

43. *Id.* at 75–76 (Holmes, J., dissenting).

44. *Id.* at 76 (Holmes, J., dissenting).

Chapter 3: The Rationalize-a-Basis Test

1. Cf. Richard Fallon, "Some Confusions About Due Process, Judicial Review, and Constitutional Remedies," 93 *Colum. L. Rev.* 309, 316 n.38 (1993) (explaining that "[f]or rationality review to be real rather than a sham, the court must be willing to make some independent assessment of legislative purpose").

2. *FCC v. Beach Commc'ns, Inc.*, 508 U.S. 307, 313, 315 (1993).

3. *United States v. Carolene Prods. Co.*, 304 U.S. 144, 152 (1938).

4. *Lewis v. Thompson*, 252 F.3d 567, 582 (2d Cir. 2001) (internal quotations omitted) (citing and quoting *Heller v. Doe*, 509 U.S. 312, 320 (1993) and *FCC v. Beach Commc'ns, Inc.*, at 315.

5. *FCC v. Beach Commc'ns, Inc.*, at 315.

6. *Haves v. City of Miami*, 52 F.3d 918, 921 (11th Cir. 1995).

Notes to pages 51–53

7. *FCC v. Beach Commc'ns, Inc.*, at 314–15 (internal quotation and citations omitted).

8. *Powers v. Harris*, 379 F.3d 1208, 1217 (10th Cir. 2004) (quoting *Starlight Sugar, Inc. v. Soto*, 253 F.3d 137, 146 (1st Cir. 2001)). See also *Flying J, Inc. v. City of New Haven*, 549 F.3d 538, 547 (7th Cir. 2008) (observing that it is "only when courts can hypothesize no rational basis for the action that allegations of animus come into play."); *Shaw v. Or. Pub. Emps.' Ret. Bd.*, 887 F.2d 947, 948 (9th Cir. 1989) (noting that "courts may properly look beyond the articulated state interest in testing a statute under the rational basis test" and explaining that "[a] court may even hypothesize the motivations of the state legislature to find a legitimate objective promoted by the provision under attack") (citations and quotation marks omitted).

9. For examples, see note 21 in Chapter 8.

10. *Edwards v. Aguillard*, 482 U.S. 578, 586–87 (1987).

11. *United States v. Virginia*, 518 U.S. 515, 533 (1996).

12. Irene Klotz, "NASA to Start Irradiating Monkeys," *Discovery*, October 29, 2009, http://news.discovery.com/space/history-of-space/space-radiation-monkeys.htm

13. *United States v. Phillips* 540 F.2d 319, 326 (8th Cir. 1976); see also *United States v. Wilgus*, 638 F.3d 1274, 1289 (10th Cir. 2011) (noting that literal application of the "least restrictive means" requirement to government action would require the government to prove a negative and explaining that "[i]n the abstract, such a thing can never be proven conclusively; the ingenuity of the human mind, especially if freed from the practical constraints of policymaking and politics, is infinite").

14. The fact that courts may, on their own initiative, dismiss a party, claim, or entire lawsuit for lack of standing or other procedural defects does not refute this point. Standing, ripeness, and other jurisdictional requirements are neutral standards that apply equally to all parties, including the government. See, e.g., *Virginia* ex rel. *Cuccinelli v. Sebelius*, 656 F.3d 253, 267–72 (4th Cir. 2011) (dismissing on standing grounds Virginia's challenge to the Patient Protection and Affordable Care Act).

15. See, e.g., *Heller v. Doe*, 509 U.S. 312, 319 (1993) (asserting that rational basis review does not "authorize the judiciary to sit as a superlegislature to judge the wisdom or desirability of legislative policy determinations made in areas that neither affect fundamental rights nor proceed along suspect lines") (internal quotation and citation omitted); *FCC v. Beach Commc'ns, Inc.* at 313 ("[E]qual protection is not a license for courts to judge the wisdom, fairness, or logic of legislative choices."). *Cf. Lochner v. New York*, 198 U.S. 45, 69 (1905) (Harlan, J., dissenting) ("Under our systems of government, the courts are not concerned with the wisdom or policy of legislation.").

16. 304 U.S. 144 (1938).

17. See, e.g., Geoffrey P. Miller, "The True Story of *Carolene Products*," 1987 *Sup. Ct. Rev.* 397, 415–22 (1987) (explaining that legislators appear to have misconstrued scientific research about the dangers of a predominately vegetable-oil-based diet and also relied on the incorrect idea that poor women used filled milk as baby formula; in an interesting twist, later studies found that filled milk is healthier than milk containing butterfat because it does not have cholesterol. *Id.* at 415).

18. *Id.* at 398.

19. *United States v. Carolene Prods. Co.*, 304 U.S. 144, 152 n.4 (1938). The text of Footnote Four reads (with case citations omitted):

> There may be narrower scope for operation of the presumption of constitutionality when legislation appears on its face to be within a specific prohibition of the Constitution, such as those of the first ten amendments . . . . It is unnecessary to consider now whether legislation which restricts those political processes which can ordinarily be expected to bring about repeal of undesirable legislation, is to be subjected to more exacting judicial scrutiny under the general prohibitions of the Fourteenth Amendment than are most other types of legislation. Nor need we enquire whether similar considerations enter into the review of statutes directed at particular religious or national or racial minorities: whether prejudice against discrete

and insular minorities may be a special condition, which tends seriously to curtail the operation of those political processes ordinarily to be relied upon to protect minorities, and which may call for a correspondingly more searching judicial inquiry.

20. *Id.* at 152 (emphasis added).

21. Miller, "The True Story of *Carolene Products*" at 399.

22. *Williamson v. Lee Optical of Oklahoma, Inc.*, 348 U.S. 483 (1955).

23. *Ferguson v. Skrupa*, 372 U.S. 726 (1963).

24. *Kotch v. Bd. of River Port Pilot Comm'rs*, 330 U.S. 552 (1947).

25. See, e.g., David E. Harrington & Jaret Treber, Institute for Justice, *Designed to Exclude: How Interior Designers Use Government Power to Exclude Minorities and Burden Consumers* (2009) (demonstrating that interior design laws reduce the number of interior designers, increase wages for government-licensed interior designers, and drive up costs for consumers).

26. The studies are collected and available at http://www.ij.org/state-interior-design-studies.

27. Joint Pretrial Stipulation at 8 ¶¶15–16, *Locke v. Shore*, No. 409cv193 (N.D. Fla. Jan. 8, 2010), available at http://www.ij.org/images/pdf_folder/first_amendment/interior_design/pretrialstipulation.pdf.

28. *Locke v. Shore*, 682 F. Supp. 2d 1283, 1290 (N.D. Fla. 2010).

29. Florida Senate Committee on Appropriations, *Senate Staff Analysis and Economic Impact Statement*, S. CS/CS/SB 127, 20th Sess., at 1–2 (1988).

30. Plaintiffs' Brief in Support of Motion for Summary Judgment at 5 n.23, *Meadows v. Odom*, 360 F. Supp. 2d 811 (M.D. La. 2005) (No. 03906B) (copy on file with the Institute for Justice).

31. *Meadows v. Odom*, 360 F. Supp. 2d 811, 813, 824 (M.D. La. 2005), *vacated as moot*, 198 Fed. Appx. 348 (5th Cir. 2005).

32. Dick M. Carpenter II, Institute for Justice, *Blooming Nonsense: Experiment Reveals Louisiana's Florist Licensing Scheme as Pointless and Anti-Competitive* 3 (2010).

33. See Plaintiffs' Brief in Support of Motion for Summary Judgment at 29 n.167, *Meadows v. Odom* (citing deposition of Bob Odom) (on file with the Institute for Justice).

34. Morris Kleiner, *Licensing Occupations: Ensuring Quality or Restricting Competition?* 1 (2006).

35. Lee McGrath, "A Primer on Occupational Licensing: With Professor Morris Kleiner," *Liberty & Law* (Institute for Justice), April 2008, at 9, available at http://ij.org/with-professor-morris-kleiner-2.

36. Kleiner, *Licensing Occupations* at 53 (citing studies from the past twenty years that the effects of licenses are uncertain, and in some situations they actually lower the level of quality for the relevant industry because the regulations "decreas[e] the total stock of practitioners").

37. Howard Baetjer Jr., *Free Our Markets: A Citizens' Guide to Essential Economics* 95–96 (forthcoming 2013).

38. My colleague Steve Simpson provides an excellent discussion of this dynamic in "Judicial Abdication and the Rise of the Special Interests," 6 *Chapman L. Rev.* 173 (2003), available at http://www.ij.org/images/pdf_folder/other_pubs/simpson_chapman_law_review.pdf.

39. See, e.g., Andrew Koppelman, "DOMA, Romer, and Rationality," 58 *Drake L. Rev.* 923, 928 (2010) (explaining that in some cases the Supreme Court "deploys what scholars have called 'rational basis with bite' to distinguish it from the toothless test that is ordinarily applied"); Kenji Yoshino, "The New Equal Protection," 124 *Harv. L. Rev.* 747, 759 (2011) (arguing that "[w]hile the Court has not made this distinction, academic commentary has correctly observed that 'rational basis review' takes two forms: ordinary rational basis review and 'rational basis with bite review'").

40. Yoshino, "The New Equal Protection," at 760. Yoshino writes (footnotes and citations omitted):

> The Supreme Court stated it would uphold state action if it could imagine any possible rationale for the state's action. In other words, even if the legislature had provided no rationale or any inadequate rationale, the state action would be upheld so long as the Court could supply one. Because judges could imagine many things, ordinary rational basis review was tantamount to a free pass for legislation.

41. 348 U.S. 483 (1955).

42. *Lee Optical of Oklahoma, Inc. v. Williamson*, 120 F. Supp. 128, 137 (W.D. Okla. 1954).

43. *Williamson v. Lee Optical of Oklahoma, Inc.*, 348 U.S. 483, 487–90 (1955).

44. 473 U.S. 432 (1985).

45. *City of Cleburne v. Cleburne Living Ctr.*, 473 U.S. 432, 448–50 (1985).

46. *Id.* at 448.

47. *Id.* at 456 (Marshall, J., dissenting).

48. *Id.* at 458 (Marshall, J., dissenting).

49. Transcript of Oral Argument at 52, *Hollingsworth v. Perry*, No. 12144 (U.S. argued Mar. 26, 2013), available at http://www.supremecourt.gov/oral_arguments/argument_transcripts/12144.pdf; Transcript of Oral Argument at 86, *United States v. Windsor*, No. 12307 (U.S. argued Mar. 27, 2013), available at http://www.supremecourt.gov/oral_arguments/argument_transcripts/12307.pdf. See also Jeffrey D. Jackson, "Putting Rationality Back into the Rational Basis Test: Saving Substantive Due Process and Redeeming the Promise of the Ninth Amendment," 45 *U. Rich. L. Rev.* 491, 538 (2011) (noting that in *Cleburne* and other "rational basis with bite" cases, the Supreme Court "professed to apply the rational basis standard, but none of the different versions of the standard employed in the cases were the same rational basis standard that *Williamson* [*v. Lee Optical*] set out").

50. Transcript of Oral Argument at 111, *United States v. Windsor*, No. 12307.

51. See, e.g., Jackson, "Putting Rationality Back into the Rational Basis Test," at 537 (arguing that "[p]roperly applied, without resort to a judicial dodge, the *Williamson* and [*FCC v.*] *Beach* standard is so toothless as to constitute no meaningful review at all; instead it essentially makes the presumption of constitutionality 'irrebutable'") (quoting Randy E. Barnett, "Scrutiny Land," 106 *Mich. L. Rev.* 1479, 1485 (2008)).

Chapter 4: A Watered-Down Constitution

1. The story about the Texas businessman's experience with eminent domain was related to the author by a partner at his former law firm in Dallas who confirmed its accuracy for this book.

2. 545 U.S. 469 (2005).

3. Jeff Benedict, *Little Pink House: A True Story of Defiance and Courage* 236 (2009). Mr. Benedict provides a detailed explanation of Ms. Gaudiani's role in the Fort Trumbull taking.

4. Robert A. Frahm, "Leave Likely for College President," *Hartford Courant*, October 7, 2000, available at http://articles.courant.com/2000-10-07/news/0010070416_1_connecticut-college-college-presidents-sabbatical.

5. Transcript of Oral Argument at 30, *Kelo v. City of New London*, 549 U.S. 469 (2005) (No. 04108), available at http://www.ij.org/images/pdf_folder/private_property/kelo/kelo_ussc_transcript.pdf.

6. *Calder v. Bull*, 3 U.S. (3 Dall.) 386, 388 (1798) (Chase, J.).

7. *Kelo v. City of New London*, 545 U.S. 469, 503 (2005) (O'Connor, J., dissenting).

8. *Id.* at 484.

9. Benedict, *Little Pink House* at 219, 129–30.

10. *Id.* at 123, 139.

11. See, e.g., Dana Berliner, Castle Coalition, *Opening the Floodgates: Eminent Domain Abuse in the Post-*Kelo *World* 2 (2006) (showing that "[t]he use of eminent domain for private development has skyrocketed" in the year following the *Kelo* decision), available at http://www.castlecoalition.org/pdf/publications/floodgates-report.pdf.

12. Castle Coalition, *Redevelopment Wrecks: 20 Failed Projects Involving Eminent Domain Abuse* (2006), available at http://castlecoalition.org/pdf/publications/Redevelopment%20Wrecks.pdf.

13. U.S. Const. art. I, § 10.

14. 290 U.S. 398 (1934).

15. See, e.g., *Home Bldg. & Loan Ass'n v. Blaisdell*, 290 U.S. 398, 427 (1934) (noting that the plight of debtors following the Revolutionary War "called forth in the States an ignoble array of legislative schemes for the defeat of creditors and the invasion of contractual obligations. Legislative interferences had been so numerous and so extreme that the confidence essential to prosperous trade had been undermined and the utter destruction of credit was threatened.").

16. Cicero, *De Officiis* [*On Obligations*], bk. II, at 261 (Walter Miller trans., Harvard University Press, Loeb Classical Library ed. 1975), quoted in Robert A. Levy & William Mellor, *The Dirty Dozen: How Twelve Supreme Court Cases Radically Expanded Government and Eroded Freedom* 54 n.9 (2008).

17. *Home Bldg. & Loan Ass'n v. Blaisdell* at 427.

18. *Id.* at 442.

19. *Id.* at 448 (Sutherland, J., dissenting).

20. *Id.* at 453 (Sutherland, J., dissenting).

21. *Id.* at 465 (Sutherland, J., dissenting).

22. Rexford G. Tugwell, "A Center Report: Rewriting the Constitution," 1 *Center Magazine* 1, 20 (1968), quoted in Roger Pilon, "The United States Constitution: From Limited Government to Leviathan," *Economic Education Bulletin* (American Institute for Economic Research), December 2005, at 1, 13–14, available at http://www.cato.org/pubs/articles/CT05.pdf.

23. See *A.L.A. Schechter Poultry Corp. v. United States*, 295 U.S. 495, 550–51 (1935).

24. *Carter v. Carter Coal Co.*, 298 U.S. 238, 295 (1936).

25. *Id.* at 295–96.

26. 317 U.S. 111 (1942).

27. On the contrary, Alexander Hamilton assured his fellow New Yorkers that even "[a]llowing the utmost latitude to the love of power which any reasonable man can require"—he's talking about congressmen—"the supervision of agriculture and of other concerns of a similar nature" would never be usurped by the federal government "because the attempt to exercise those powers would be as troublesome as it would be nugatory." *The Federalist* No. 17, at 118–19 (Alexander Hamilton) (Clinton Rossiter ed., 1961).

28. *Wickard v. Filburn*, 317 U.S. 111, 127–28 (1942).

29. 545 U.S. 1 (2005).

30. 132 S. Ct. 2566 (2012).

31. Ms. Raich's medical conditions are described on her personal website and in the sworn declaration she filed in support of her lawsuit challenging the federal marijuana ban. "Who Is Angel McClary Raich?" Angel Raich's

Website, http://www.angeljustice.org/angel/Who_is_Angel_Raich.html; Declaration of Angel McClary Raich in Support of Preliminary Injunction at 1–18, *Raich v. Ashcroft*, 248 F. Supp. 2d 918 (N.D. Cal. 2003) (No. C 02-4872 MJJ), *vacated sub nom. Gonzales v. Raich*, 545 U.S. 1 (2005), available (as "Declaration of Angel McClary Raich, October 25, 2002") at http://www.angeljustice.org/angel/Who_is_Angel_Raich.html.

32. "Who Is Angel McClary Raich?" Angel Raich's Website.

33. *Gonzales v. Raich*, 545 U.S. 1, 13, 16 (2005).

34. *United States v. Lopez*, 514 U.S. 549 (1995) (striking down the Gun Free School Zones Act of 1990); *United States v. Morrison*, 529 U.S. 598 (2000) (striking down the provision of the Violence Against Women Act that created a federal civil remedy for victims of gender-motivated violence). Following the *Lopez* decision, Congress amended the Gun Free School Zones Act to include a jurisdictional element requiring the government to show that the gun in question "has moved in or . . . otherwise affects interstate or foreign commerce." See 18 U.S.C. § 922(q)(3)(A) (2013). Federal appellate courts have so far upheld the law as amended, and the Supreme Court has not reviewed any of those decisions. See, e.g., *United States v. Nieves-Castano*, 480 F.3d 597 (1st Cir. 2007) (ruling against the petitioner's claim that the statute's method of measuring the distance from the school to her home was unconstitutionally vague); *United States v. Dorsey*, 418 F.3d 1038 (9th Cir. 2005) (holding that the revised Gun Free School Zones Act was constitutional); *United States v. Danks*, 221 F.3d 1037 (8th Cir. 1999), *cert. denied sub nom. Danks v. United States*, 528 U.S. 1091 (2000) (dismissing the petitioner's claim that the revised statute violated the commerce clause power); *United States v. Smith*, 182 F.3d 452 (6th Cir. 1999), *cert. denied sub nom. Smith v. United States*, 530 U.S. 1206 (2000) (holding that even though the effects on interstate commerce were de minimis, the statute still applied).

35. *Nat'l Fed'n of Indep. Bus. v. Sebelius*, 132 S. Ct. 2566, 2588 (2012).

36. *Id.*

37. *Id.*

38. See, e.g., Robert Pear, "Changing Stance, Administration Now Defends Insurance Mandate as a Tax," *New York Times*, July 18, 2010, at A14, available

at http://www.nytimes.com/2010/07/18/health/policy/18health.html?_r=0.
According to the article, Yale law professor Jack M. Balkin, a noted progressive and a supporter of Obamacare, said that Obama "'has not been honest
with the American people about the nature of [the Affordable Care Act].'"
According to Balkin, the individual mandate is a tax. And "'[b]ecause it's a
tax, it's completely constitutional.'"

39. *Nat'l Fed'n of Indep. Bus. v. Sebelius* at 2593 (emphasis added).

40. *Id.* at 2594 (internal quotations and citations omitted).

41. *Florida v. U.S. Dep't of Health & Human Servs.*, 716 F. Supp. 2d 1120, 1143
(N.D. Fla. 2010), *aff'd in part and rev'd in part*, 648 F.3d 1235 (11th Cir. 2011),
aff'd in part and rev'd in part, 132 S. Ct. 2566 (2012).

42. *Zobel v. Williams*, 457 U.S. 55 (1982) (holding that the Alaska legislature's
plan to assign dividends to state residents based on the length of their residency violated the right to interstate travel); *Mem'l Hosp. v. Maricopa Cnty.*, 415
U.S. 250 (1974) (ruling that a state statute granting free medical treatment to
indigent people, which was based on residency length, was unconstitutional);
Pierce v. Soc'y of Sisters, 268 U.S. 510 (1925) (stating that parents have a liberty
interest in educating and raising their children); *Meyer v. Nebraska*, 262 U.S.
390 (1923) (ruling that parents have a liberty interest in teaching their children
foreign languages).

43. Randy E. Barnett, "Scrutiny Land," 106 *Mich. L. Rev.* 1479, 1479 (2008).

44. 521 U.S. 702 (1997).

45. *Washington v. Glucksberg*, 521 U.S. 702, 720–21 (1997) (internal quotations
and citations omitted).

46. 495 F.3d 695 (D.C. Cir. 2007) (en banc).

47. *Abigail Alliance for Better Access to Developmental Drugs v. Eschenbach*, 495 F.3d
695, 701 (D.C. Cir. 2007) (en banc).

48. *Id.* at 714 (Rogers and Ginsburg, JJ., dissenting).

49. *Id.* at 716 (Rogers and Ginsburg, JJ., dissenting).

50. *Id.* at 722 (Rogers and Ginsburg, JJ., dissenting).

51. See, e.g., *ACLU v. Alvarez*, 679 F.3d 583, 609 (7th Cir. 2012) (Posner,
J., dissenting) (dissenting from a decision finding that state law making it a
felony to audio-record public conversations likely violates the First Amend-

ment and arguing that "[t]he invalidation of a statute on constitutional grounds should be a rare and solemn judicial act, done with reluctance under compulsion of clear binding precedent or clear constitutional language or—in the absence of those traditional sources of guidance—compelling evidence, or an overwhelming gut feeling, that the statute has intolerable consequences").

Chapter 5: Liberty Slaughtered

1. In North Carolina, for example, an abolitionist named Daniel Worth was indicted for circulating *The Impending Crisis*, an antislavery tract that doubled as a Republican campaign document, and sentenced to twelve months in prison. *State v. Worth*, 52 N.C. 488, 492–94 (1860). Virginia criminalized the act of outsiders' "advocat[ing] or advis[ing] the abolition of slavery." See Clement Eaton, *The Freedom of Thought in the Old South* 127, 245 (1940).

2. *Barron v. Baltimore*, 32 U.S. 243 (1833).

3. House Ex. Doc. No. 70, 39th Cong., 1st Sess., at 236–39 (1866).

4. See David T. Hardy, "Original Popular Understanding of the Fourteenth Amendment as Reflected in the Print Media of 1866–68," 30 *Whittier L. Rev.* 695, 703–07 (2009), available at http://papers.ssrn.com/sol3/papers.cfm?abstract_id=1322323.

5. Civil Rights Act of 1866, 14 Stat. 27.

6. U.S. Const. amend. XIV, § 1.

7. See, e.g., Michael Kent Curtis, *No State Shall Abridge: The Fourteenth Amendment and the Bill of Rights* 64–65 (1986) (noting that the "words rights, liberties, privileges, and immunities, seem to have been used interchangeably.").

8. See, e.g., U.S. Const. amend. IX ("The enumeration in the Constitution, of certain rights, shall not be construed to deny or disparage others retained by the people.").

9. *Slaughter-House Cases*, 83 U.S. (16 Wall.) 36 (1873).

10. *Id.* at 59–60.

11. *Id.* at 66–67.

12. *Id.* at 60.

13. *Id.*

14. *Id.* at 78–80.

15. Compare *id.* at 75 (misquoting the text of Article IV's privileges and immunities clause) with *id.* at 117 (Bradley, J., dissenting) (explaining the significance of Justice Miller's misquotation). The significance of Justice Miller's misquotation of Article IV is discussed in Curtis, *No State Shall Abridge* at 175–76.

16. *Slaughter-House Cases* at 77–78.

17. *Id.* at 96 (Field, J., dissenting).

18. *Id.* at 122 (Bradley, J., dissenting).

19. *Id.* at 129 (Swayne, J., dissenting).

20. Richard L. Aynes, "Constricting the Law of Freedom: Justice Miller, the Fourteenth Amendment, and the Slaughter-House Cases," 70 *Chi.-Kent L. Rev.* 627, 627 (1994). See also 1 Laurence H. Tribe, *American Constitutional Law* § 7–6 (3d ed. 2000) ("[T]he textual and historical case for treating the Privileges or Immunities Clause as the primary source of federal protection against state rights-infringement is very powerful indeed."); Akhil Reed Amar, *The Bill of Rights: Creation and Reconstruction* 212–13 (1998) (explaining "[t]he obvious inadequacy of Miller's opinion—on virtually any reading of the Fourteenth Amendment" in *Slaughter-House*).

21. Eric Foner, *Reconstruction: America's Unfinished Revolution, 1863–1877*, at 503 (1988).

22. Thomas B. McAffee, "Constitutional Interpretation—the Uses and Limitations of Original Intent," 12 *U. Dayton L. Rev.* 275, 282 (1986).

23. 554 U.S. 570 (2008).

24. *McDonald v. City of Chicago*, 130 S. Ct. 3020, 3058–88 (2010) (Thomas, J., concurring).

25. See *id.* at 3028–31 (Alito, J.); *id.* at 3089 (Stevens, J., dissenting).

26. *Id.* at 3029–31 (Alito, J.).

27. *Id.* at 3030 (Alito, J.) (quoting Akhil R. Amar, "Substance and Method in the Year 2000," 18 *Pepperdine L. Rev.* 601, 631 n.178 (2001) and Brief for Constitutional Law Professors as *Amici Curiae* Supporting Petitioners, *McDonald v. City of Chicago*, 130 S. Ct. 3020 (2010) at 33).

28. For a thoughtful discussion of how Fourteenth Amendment jurisprudence might look different today had the Supreme Court not misread the privileges or immunities clause in *Slaughter-House*, see Kermit Roosevelt III, "What if *Slaughter-House* Had Been Decided Differently?" 45 *Ind. L. Rev.* 61 (2011).

29. *McDonald v. City of Chicago* at 3050 (Scalia, J., concurring).

30. *Id.*

31. Compare, e.g., A. Christopher Bryant, "What *McDonald* Means for Unenumerated Rights," 45 *Ga. L. Rev.* 1073 (2013) (explaining that "[f]ar from undermining the application of (most of) the Bill of Rights to the states, a Privileges or Immunities ruling may have placed the practice on a firmer foundation, while at the same time making less radical the consequences of adopting the interpretive method Scalia professes to embrace") with Robert Bork, *The Tempting of America* 166 (1997) (likening the Fourteenth Amendment's privileges or immunities clause to an ink blot).

Chapter 6: Why Do Judges Abdicate?

1. See, e.g., Randy E. Barnett, "Judicial Engagement Through the Lens of *Lee Optical*," 19 *Geo. Mason L. Rev.* 845, 857 (2012) (critiquing the Supreme Court's application of rational basis review in *Williamson v. Lee Optical* and explaining that "[f]or all practical purposes, what had once been a true presumption that was rebuttable by evidence and reasoning would henceforth be an irrebuttable presumption, which is not truly a presumption at all").

2. 545 U.S. 469 (2005).

3. Owners of beachfront homes in Long Branch, New Jersey, were threatened with eminent domain in 2005. The town planned to transfer the properties to a developer who would replace the modest bungalows with multi-story condominiums. The town claimed the homes were blighted, but after several years of litigation it dismissed the eminent domain action. See Institute for Justice Litigation Backgrounder, "Eminent Domain Abuse in Long Branch, N.J.," http://www.ij.org/long-branch-nj-eminent-domain-background; Institute for Justice Web Release, "Victory for Homeowners in Long Branch,

N.J. Eminent Domain Battle," September 15, 2009, available at http://www. ij.org/victory-for-homeowners-in-long-branch-nj-eminent-domain-battle.

In 2001, the city of Mesa, Arizona, tried to condemn small-business owner Randy Bailey's brake shop so it could give the land to another business. The Arizona Court of Appeals ruled that transferring property from one private business to another was not a public use under the state analogue to the Fifth Amendment's public use provision. See Institute for Justice Litigation Backgrounder, "Putting the Brakes on Eminent Domain Abuse in Mesa, Arizona," http://www.ij.org/mesa-arizona-background; *Bailey v. Myers*, 206 Ariz. 224 (Ariz. Ct. App. 2003).

4. 467 U.S. 229 (1984).

5. *Kelo v. City of New London*, 545 U.S. 469, 503 (2005) (O'Connor, J., dissenting).

6. 317 U.S. 111 (1942).

7. *Locke v. Shore*, 634 F.3d 1185, 1191 (11th Cir. 2011).

8. *Hettinga v. United States*, 677 F.3d 471, 475 (D.C. Cir. 2012).

9. *Id.* at 480 (Brown, J., and Sentelle, C.J., concurring).

10. *Id.* at 481 (Brown, J., and Sentelle, C.J., concurring).

11. *Id.* (quoting *Nebbia v. New York*, 291 U.S. 502, 523 (1934) (McReynolds, J., dissenting)).

12. *Id.* at 482 (Brown, J., and Sentelle, C.J., concurring).

13. *Id.* at 482–83 (Brown, J., and Sentelle, C.J., concurring).

14. *Id.* at 483 (Griffith, J., concurring).

15. James M. Buchanan, "Politics Without Romance: A Sketch of Positive Public Choice Theory and Its Normative Implications," in *The Theory of Public Choice–II*, at 11 (James M. Buchanan & Robert D. Tollison eds., 1984).

16. Robert Pear, "If Only Laws Were Like Sausages," *New York Times*, December 4, 2010, at WK3, available at http://www.nytimes.com/2010/12/05/weekinreview/05pear.html?_r=1&.

17. See, e.g., Ilya Somin, "Deliberative Democracy and Political Ignorance," 22 *Critical Review* 253, 257–62 (2010) (explaining concept of "rational ignorance" on the part of voters), available at http://papers.ssrn.com/sol3/papers.cfm?abstract_id=1694650.

18. See Maxwell L. Stearns & Todd J. Zywicki, *Public Choice Concepts and Applications in Law* 46–51 (2009).

19. Jack Abramoff, *Capitol Punishment: The Hard Truth About Washington Corruption From America's Most Notorious Lobbyist* 63 (2011).

20. William F. Shugart II, "Public Choice," in *The Concise Encyclopedia of Economics* (David R. Henderson ed., 2d ed. 2008), available at http://www.econlib.org/library/Enc/PublicChoice.html.

21. *Williamson v. Lee Optical of Oklahoma, Inc.*, 348 U.S. 483, 488 (1955) (internal quotation and citations omitted).

22. See, e.g., Jonathan T. Molot, "Ambivalence About Formalism," 93 *Va. L. Rev.* 1, 16–19 (2007) (describing constitutional minimalist theory and noting of its adherents that "[t]hey focus instead upon getting judges to tread lightly and to leave as much as possible for the political process to resolve"). See also J. Harvie Wilkinson III, "Of Guns, Abortion, and the Unraveling Rule of Law," 95 *Va. L. Rev.* 253, 288–89 (2009) (arguing that instead of the Court deciding cases involving "complex inquiries best left to the political process," it should "honor the structure of our constitution, stay out of the thicket, and leave the highly motivated contestants in this field to press their agendas in the political process where the issue properly belongs and where for centuries it has remained"); Arthur D. Hellman, "Judicial Activism: The Good, the Bad, and the Ugly," 21 *Miss. C. L. Rev.* 253, 261 (2002) ("[B]y resolving ambiguities in regulatory statutes in favor of the status quo, the Court would allow the better-equipped political process to determine the nature and extent of change as well as the limits of the new obligation.").

23. *Hettinga v. United States* at 483 (Brown, J., and Sentelle, C.J., concurring).

24. Matthew Mosk, "Law on Md. Mortuaries Has Guardian Angel at State House," *Washington Post*, January 4, 2006, at A1.

25. *Brown v. Hovatter*, 561 F.3d 357, 369 (4th Cir. 2009) (quoting *Williamson v. Lee Optical of Oklahoma, Inc.*, 348 U.S. 483, 488 (1955)) (emphasis added).

26. Robert H. Bork, *The Tempting of America: The Political Seduction of the Law* 139 (1990).

27. *FCC v. Beach Commc'ns, Inc.*, 508 U.S. 307, 315 (1993).

28. See, e.g., *Armour v. City of Indianapolis*, 132 S. Ct. 2073, 2080 (2012).

29. Institute for Justice Litigation Backgrounder, "Texas Government-Mandated Computer Repair License Does Not Compute," http://www.ij.org/texas-computer-repair-background (describing lawsuit challenging a Texas law that required people who perform certain computer repairs to have a private investigator's license).

30. Richard A. Posner, "The Rise and Fall of Judicial Self-Restraint," 100 *Calif. L. Rev.* 519, 522 (2012) (quoting James B. Thayer, "The Origin and Scope of the American Doctrine of Constitutional Law," 7 *Harv. L. Rev.* 129, 144 (1893)).

31. Randy E. Barnett, "Who's Afraid of Unenumerated Rights?" 9 *U. Pa. J. Const. L.* 1, 6 (2006).

32. David E. Bernstein, *Rehabilitating* Lochner: *Defending Individual Rights against Progressive Reform* 70 (price controls), 78 (residential segregation), 96–98 (eugenics) (2011).

33. Posner, "The Rise and Fall of Judicial Self-Restraint," at 537.

34. See, e.g., Timothy Sandefur, "The Wolves and the Sheep of Constitutional Law: A Review Essay on Kermit Roosevelt's *The Myth of Judicial Activism*," 23 *J.L. & Pol.* 1, 17 (2007).

35. J. Harvie Wilkinson III, "Of Guns, Abortion, and the Unraveling Rule of Law," 95 *Va. L. Rev.* 253, 255 (2009) (emphasis added).

36. See, e.g., Lino A. Graglia, "'Interpreting' the Constitution: Posner on Bork," 44 *Stan. L. Rev.* 1019, 1044 (1992) ("Judicial invalidation of the elected representatives' policy choices should be permitted only when (as would very rarely be the case) the choice is clearly disallowed by the Constitution."). This position has attracted prominent liberal scholars as well in recent years. See, e.g., Cass R. Sunstein, "Debate on Radicals in Robes," in *Originalism: A Quarter-Century of Debate* 287, 313 (Stephen G. Calabresi ed., 2007) ("[T]he Constitution should be invoked to disable the democratic process, only when it plainly does so.") (internal quotation and citation omitted); Jeffrey Rosen, "Are Liberals Trying to Intimidate John Roberts?" *New Republic*, May 28, 2012, www.newrepublic.com/article/politics/103656/obamacare-affordable-care-act-critics-response ("[R]estraint requires deference to all laws passed by Congress and the states, regardless of whether they're favored by liberals

or conservatives, unless they violate principles that can be so clearly located in constitutional text and history that people of all political persuasions can readily accept them.").

37. U.S. Const. amend. II.

38. Kermit Roosevelt III, *The Myth of Judicial Activism: Making Sense of Supreme Court Decisions* 38 (2006).

39. U.S. Const. amend. XIV, § 1.

40. Bork, *The Tempting of America* at 166. As Professor Richard Aynes, a leading scholar of the privileges or immunities clause, notes, "Judge Bork apparently did not work very hard in his attempt to discover its meaning." Richard L. Aynes, "Ink Blot or Not: The Meaning of Privileges and/or Immunities," 11 *U. Pa. J. Const. L.* 1295, 1300 n.34 (2009).

41. For an illustration of this point, compare the plurality and dissenting opinions in *McDonald v. City of Chicago*, 130 S. Ct. 3020 (2010), which contain no meaningful discussion of the privileges or immunities clause, with Justice Thomas's concurring opinion, *id.* at 3058–88, which carefully examines the relevant history and argues persuasively that the privileges or immunities clause was designed to protect an array of individual rights, including the right to own a gun.

Chapter 7: The Judicial Activism Bogeyman

1. John Marini, "Abandoning the Constitution," 12 *Claremont Review of Books* 27, 30 (2012).

2. See, e.g., *We the People? Corporate Spending in American Elections after Citizens United*, Hearing Before the Senate Committee on the Judiciary, March 10, 2010, 111th Cong., at 30 (statement of Jeffrey Rosen, Professor of Law, George Washington University) (asserting that "[*Citizens United*] is activist by any definition of activism" because of the Court's refusal to defer to the other branches of government as well as precedent); Mark R. Levin, *Men in Black: How the Supreme Court Is Destroying America* 118–23 (2005) (referring to *Rasul v. Bush* and *Hamdi v. Rumsfeld* as "egregious examples of judicial activism" for allowing alleged terrorists to challenge their incarceration); Stephen G. Calabresi, "*Lawrence*, the Fourteenth Amendment, and the Supreme Court's

Reliance on Foreign Constitutional Law: An Originalist Appeal," 65 *Ohio St. L.J.* 1097, 1100 (2004) (while claiming that *"Lawrence* is a far less activist decision than *Roe,"* asserting still that *"Lawrence* is a clear victory for the forces of judicial activism"); Jeffrey Toobin, "Precedent and Prologue," *New Yorker,* December 2010, at 27, available at http://www.newyorker.com/talk/comment/2010/12/06/101206taco_talk_toobin (characterizing *Bush v. Gore* as "a classic example of judicial activism, not judicial restraint, by the majority"); Jack M. Balkin, "History Lesson," *Legal Affairs,* July/August 2002, at 44, 44–49, available at http://www.legalaffairs.org/issues/July-August-2002/review_balkin_julaug2002.msp (referring to the Rehnquist Court's striking down of federal laws, in such cases as *United States v. Morrison,* as "new conservative judicial activism" that flies in the face of the precedent of federal laws protecting civil rights); Erwin Chemerinsky, "The *Heller* Decision: Conservative Activism and Its Aftermath," *Cato Unbound,* July 25, 2008, http://www.cato-unbound.org/2008/07/25/erwin-chemerinsky/the-heller-decision-conservative-activism-and-its-aftermath/ (in striking down the D.C. handgun ban, the five majority justices "showed that the conservative rhetoric about judicial restraint is a guise that is used to oppose rights they don't like. When it serves their political agenda, conservatives, such as Justice Scalia, are very much the activists.").

3.   See, e.g., Levin, *Men in Black* at 22, 33, 53, 205–08; John Thomas Tucker, "Tyranny of the Judiciary: Judicial Dilution of Consent Under Section 2 of the Voting Rights Act," 7 *Wm. & Mary Bill Rts. J.* 443 (1993); Kevin R. C. Gutzman, "Tyranny of the Judiciary: Under the Guise of Following the Constitution, Our Legal Elites Usurp It," *American Conservative,* April 20, 2012, http://www.theamericanconservative.com/articles/tyranny-of-the-judiciary/; Edward L. Daley, "The Growing Tyranny of the Judiciary," *American Thinker,* July 22, 2004, available at http://www.americanthinker.com/2004/07/the_growing_tyranny_of_the_jud.html. Similar phrases, such as "judicial tyranny," are also widely used. For example, see Mark I. Sutherland et al., *Judicial Tyranny: The New Kings of America?* (2005); Carrol D. Kilgore, *Judicial Tyranny: An Inquiry into the Integrity of the Federal Judiciary* (1977); Steven W. Fitschen, "Impeaching Federal Judges: A Covenantal and Constitutional Response to Judicial Tyranny," 10 *Regent U. L. Rev.* 111 (1998).

4. 554 U.S. 570, 599 (2008).

5. *Citizens United v. Fed. Elections Comm'n*, 558 U.S. 310 (2010). See also Clint Bolick, *David's Hammer: The Case for an Activist Judiciary* ix (2007) ("[I]ncreasingly, many today on both the right and the left define judicial activism . . . as the act of courts striking down laws enacted by the democratic branches."); Jeffrey Toobin, "Money Unlimited: How Chief Justice John Roberts Orchestrated the *Citizens United* Decision," *New Yorker*, May 12, 2012, http://www.newyorker.com/reporting/2012/05/21/120521fa_fact_toobin (claiming that the decision in *Citizens United* "reflects the aggressive conservative judicial activism of the Roberts Court" and that "Anthony Kennedy . . . was reshaping American politics"). The idea that a deferential Supreme Court is a nonactivist Court is widespread within the legal community. Judge J. Harvie Wilkinson of the Fourth Circuit characterized *District of Columbia v. Heller* as an activist decision because the Court did not show enough deference to the other branches of government. J. Harvie Wilkinson III, "Of Guns, Abortions, and the Unraveling Rule of Law," 95 *Va. L. Rev.* 253 (2009) (arguing that by striking down the disputed gun statute in *District of Columbia v. Heller*, the Court violated the principles of federalism and restricted the ability of legislatures to make new laws, and that "[t]he resulting law might still be poor policy, but a representative government has the right to make that call"). Similarly, Professor Cass Sunstein believes that "it is best to measure judicial activism by seeing how often a court strikes down the actions of other parts of government, especially Congress." Cass R. Sunstein, *Radicals in Robes: Why Extreme Right-Wing Courts Are Wrong for America* 15 (2005), quoted in Marcilynn A. Burke, "Much Ado About Nothing: *Kelo v. City of New London, Babbitt v. Sweet Home*, and Other Tales from the Supreme Court," 75 *U. Cin. L. Rev.* 663, 712–13 (2006); see also Jeffrey Rosen, "The Unregulated Offensive," *New York Times Magazine*, April 17, 2005, available at http://www.nytimes.com/2005/04/17/magazine/17CONSTITUTION.html?pagewanted=print&position= (concluding that many conservative and libertarian-leaning judges and legal scholars are "thwart[ing] the will of the people" by not giving deference to the other branches). One possible reason that this is a popular theory regarding activism, according to Kermit

Roosevelt, is that "[a] judge who upholds a law can hardly be accused of imposing his views." Kermit Roosevelt III, *The Myth of Judicial Activism: Making Sense of Supreme Court Decisions* 39 (2006).

Those who agree with this interpretation of judicial activism also support the majority opinion in *Kelo v. City of New London* because the Court did the exact opposite from *Heller*—it upheld the city's decisions and accepted the asserted rationale for its actions. In particular, Justice Stevens, the author of that opinion, maintains that the Court properly deferred to the other branches and exercised proper restraint. John Paul Stevens, "*Kelo*, Popularity, and Substantive Due Process," 63 *Ala. L. Rev.* 941 (2012).

6. Lino A. Graglia, "It's Not Constitutionalism, It's Judicial Activism," 19 *Harv. J.L. & Pub. Pol'y* 293, 296 (1996), quoted in Keenan D. Kmiec, Comment, "The Origin and Current Meanings of 'Judicial Activism,'" 92 *Calif. L. Rev.* 1441, 1464 (2004). See also Craig Green, "An Intellectual History of Judicial Activism," 58 *Emory L.J.* 1195, 1227 (2009) (noting that "[m]any scholars have claimed that judicial activism is identified by inadequate respect for Congress or the executive branch") and *id.* at 1217 n.88 (noting Judge Richard Posner's observation that "a basic element of judicial activism is the willingness to act 'contrary to the will of the other branches of government,' such as striking down a statute") (quoting Richard A. Posner, *The Federal Courts: Challenge and Reform* 320 (1996)).

7. But see Roosevelt, *The Myth of Judicial Activism*.

8. "Bogeyman," Wikipedia, http://en.wikipedia.org/wiki/Bogeyman.

9. President Barack Obama, Joint Press Conference by President Obama, President Calderon of Mexico, and Prime Minister Harper of Canada, April 2, 2012, available at http://www.whitehouse.gov/the-press-office/2012/04/02/joint-press-conference-president-obama-president-calderon-mexico-and-pri; Jeffrey M. Jones, "Americans Divided on Repeal of 2010 Healthcare Law," *Gallup Politics*, February 27, 2012, http://www.gallup.com/poll/152969/americans-divided-repeal-2010-healthcare-law.aspx.

10. *Hearing on the Nomination of John G. Roberts, Jr. to Be Chief Justice of the United States*, Hearing Before the Senate Committee on the Judiciary, September 12–15, 2005, 109th Cong., at 49 (statement of Sen. Tom Coburn, Member,

S. Comm. on the Judiciary). A transcript of the Roberts confirmation hearing is available at http://www.washingtonpost.com/wp-dyn/content/article/2005/09/13/AR2005091300693.html.

11. *Id.* at 30 (statement of Sen. Jeff Sessions, Member, S. Comm. on the Judiciary).

12. *Id.* at 25 (statement of Sen. Mike DeWine, Member, S. Comm. on the Judiciary).

13. *Id.* at 46 (statement of Sen. Sam Brownback, Member, S. Comm. on the Judiciary).

14. *Id.* at 158 (statement of John G. Roberts, Jr.).

15. E.g., *The Nomination of Elena Kagan to Be an Associate Justice of the Supreme Court of the United States*, Hearing Before the Senate Committee on the Judiciary, June 28–July 1, 2010, 111th Cong., at 27 (statement of Sen. Charles E. Schumer, Member, S. Comm. on the Judiciary) ("I am concerned that we will soon find ourselves back in the Lochner era of activist judging.").

16. *Id.* at 266 (statement of Sen. Lindsey Graham, Member, S. Comm. on the Judiciary) ("So, what is your definition of an 'activist judge'? . . . Can you name one person in the United States that you think would be an activist judge, living or dead?").

17. *Id.* at 31 (statement of Sen. John Cornyn, Member, S. Comm. on the Judiciary).

18. *Id.* at 57 (statement of Elena Kagan, Solicitor General of the United States).

19. The number for each term reflects its use in statements expressing either concern about judicial activism or the need for a more restrained Court. Terms were not counted when their use was not directly related to such contexts.

20. *Confirmation Hearing on the Nomination of Samuel A. Alito, Jr. to Be an Associate Justice of the Supreme Court of the United States*, Hearing Before the Senate Committee on the Judiciary, January 9–13, 2006, 109th Cong., at 4 (statement of Sen. Arlen Specter, Chairman, S. Comm. on the Judiciary).

21. 156 *Cong. Rec.* S10,854 (2010) (farewell address of Sen. Arlen Specter) (emphases added).

22.   See Toby Hyde, "Upper Levels Sunday: Good Starts from Jeurys Familia and Collin McHugh," Mets Minor League Blog, April 23, 2012, http:// metsminorleagueblog.com/buffalo-bisons/upper-levels-sunday-good-starts-from-jeurys-familia-and-collin-mchugh/ ("He threw 63.5% of his pitches for strikes (MLB average is 62%)."). Toby Hyde is the director of broadcasting and communications for the Savannah Sand Gnats.

23.   Clark Neily & Dick M. Carpenter II, Institute for Justice, *Government Unchecked: The False Problem of "Judicial Activism" and the Need for Judicial Engagement* 1 (2011), available at http://www.ij.org/images/pdf_folder/other_pubs/ grvnmtunchkd.pdf.

24.   While it is true that the Supreme Court can hear only so many cases every year, the Court's docket has been steadily shrinking even as government at all levels has been expanding. See Adam Liptak, "The Case of the Plummeting Supreme Court Docket," *New York Times*, September 29, 2009, at A18, available at http://www.nytimes.com/2009/09/29/us/29bar.html?_r=0 (reporting that while "[i]n the early 1980s the Supreme Court decided more than 150 cases a year . . . it decides about half that many" now); see also "History of the Federal Judiciary," Federal Judicial Center, http://www.fjc.gov/history/ caseload.nsf/page/caseloads_petitions_for_certiorari_2 (reporting a similar decline in petitions for certiorari granted since the 1980s). Speaking publicly at the 2012 Judicial Conference for the District of Columbia Circuit, on June 29, Chief Justice Roberts said he believed the Supreme Court could hear as many as "100 cases without any stress or strain, but the cases just aren't there." The Supreme Court routinely denies certiorari in constitutional cases challenging the exercise of government power, but not because there is no room on its docket to hear them.

25.   Kermit Roosevelt III, *The Myth of Judicial Activism: Making Sense of Supreme Court Decisions* 41–42 (2006).

26.   See *id.* at 3–4. As a rhetorical antidote to the ad hominem term "activism," Roosevelt introduces the concept of "legitimacy," by which he means decisions by the Supreme Court that are, whether rightly or wrongly decided, intellectually defensible applications of constitutional text "in terms of deferring

or not deferring to the government body whose action it is reviewing." *Id.* at 3. Applying that standard and "mov[ing] beyond the misleadingly simplistic rhetoric of activism," Roosevelt argues that "most Supreme Court decisions are in fact legitimate." *Id.* at 3–4.

I agree with that conclusion as to decisions in which the Supreme Court has restricted government, because I believe there are few areas in which the Constitution permits government to act with unfettered discretion. But the use of rational basis review and other forms of make-believe judging casts doubt on the legitimacy of many decisions upholding government action, for reasons explained in this book.

27. See, e.g., *id.* at 15 (noting that "[m]ost critics start out by saying that the decisions they call activist are wrong. But activism is more than error, and the next step is thus to argue that the error is so blatant that it cannot be a good faith mistake; it must be the deliberate imposition of the judge's own preferences in defiance of the Constitution"); Craig Green, "An Intellectual History of Judicial Activism," 58 *Emory L.J.* 1195, 1198 n.3 (2009) (calling the term "activism" "the utmost judicial putdown" (quoting Stephen F. Smith, "Activism as Restraint: Lessons from Criminal Procedure," 80 *Tex. L. Rev.* 1057, 1077 (2002)); see also *id.* at 1219 n.92 (explaining that judicial activism is "'always an insult'" (quoting Cass R. Sunstein, *Radicals in Robes: Why Extreme Right-Wing Courts Are Wrong for America* 42 (2005)); Keenan D. Kmiec, Comment, "The Origin and Current Meanings of 'Judicial Activism,'" 92 *Calif. L. Rev.* 1441, 1464 (2004) (urging that "'judicial activism' cannot be synonymous with merely exercising judicial review").

28. *The Federalist* No. 45, at 292 (James Madison) (Clinton Rossiter ed., 1961).

29. See U.S. Const. amend. IX ("The enumeration in the Constitution, of certain rights, shall not be construed to deny or disparage others retained by the people.").

30. See U.S. Const. amend. XIV, § 1, cls.2–4 ("No State shall make or enforce any law which shall abridge the privileges or immunities of citizens of the United States; nor shall any State deprive any person of life, liberty, or property, without due process of law; nor deny to any person within its jurisdiction the equal protection of the laws.").

Chapter 8: Real Judging in All Constitutional Cases

1. Because Mars and the outer planets occupy more distant orbits than Earth, they appear to move backward at certain times during the year, when Earth comes around the turn like a sprinter on the inside lane of a track whipping past her competitors on the outside lanes. In putting Earth stationary in the center of the solar system, Greek and medieval astronomers had to explain this apparent backward ("retrograde") motion of the outer planets some other way, which they did by hypothesizing that those planets make "epicycles"—essentially an orbital loop-the-loop—at certain points in their rotation through the geocentric solar system.

2. *ACLU v. Alvarez*, 679 F.3d 583, 586 (7th Cir. 2012) (citing 720 Ill. Comp. Stat. 5/141(d), 5/142(a)(1) & 5/144(b) (2012)); *id.* at 592 & n.2.

3. See generally Steven A. Lautt, Note,"Sunlight Is Still the Best Disinfectant: The Case for a First Amendment Right to Record the Police," 51 *Washburn L. Rev.* 349, 355–60 (2012) (discussing and documenting use of catchall charges to discourage people from recording police officers in public).

In May 2012, the Department of Justice sent a strongly worded letter to the Baltimore Police Department regarding an incident in which officers seized and deleted the contents of Christopher Sharp's cell phone while he was using it to record the arrest of a friend. The letter explains that citizens have a constitutional right to record police officers in public and urges the Baltimore Police Department to adopt specific training requirements to ensure that its officers respect that right in the future. The letter is available at http://www.justice.gov/crt/about/spl/documents/Sharp_ltr_5-14-12.pdf.

The Cato Institute prepared a short video, in which the author appears, regarding the issue of recording police officers in public: http://www.youtube.com/watch?v=tE8Xom38Rd8.

4. Although it is nearly impossible to find any examples of prosecutions involving only private parties, prosecutions of citizens for recording police officers and other public officials abound. See, e.g., *ACLU v. Alvarez*, 679 F.3d 583, 592 n.2 (7th Cir. 2012) (listing examples of people prosecuted for recording police officers in public); Roslyn Anderson, "Twins Allegedly Arrested for Recording Police Shooting," *MS News Now*, February 19, 2013,

http://www.msnewsnow.com/story/18074344/twins-allegedly-arrested-for-recording-police-shooting (reporting how two teenagers were verbally assaulted, manhandled, and arrested for recording a shooting on a cell phone; the first teen was arrested for filming the shooting, and the second teen was thrown to the ground after questioning her brother's arrest); Radley Balko, "Chicago State's Attorney Lets Bad Cops Slide, Prosecutes Citizens Who Record Them," *Huffington Post*, August 8, 2011, http://www.huffingtonpost.com/2011/06/08/chicago-district-attorney-recording-bad-cops_n_872921.html (detailing the arrest of a woman who recorded her conversations with internal affairs officers who tried to discourage her for pursuing a complaint against another officer she had accused of sexually assaulting her); Annys Shin, "Traffic Stop Video on YouTube Sparks Debate on Police Use of Md. Wiretap Laws," *Washington Post*, June 16, 2010, http://www.washingtonpost.com/wp-dyn/content/article/2010/06/15/AR2010061505556.html?sid=ST2010061505592 (describing unsuccessful prosecution of motorcyclist who faced sixteen-year prison sentence for recording a traffic stop with his helmet camera).

While the government will put ordinary citizens in jail for several years for this offense, it appears that there might be special treatment when elected officials violate the same laws. Last fall, Chicago city officials admitted to recording journalists during interviews without first seeking their consent. Even though it is illegal in Illinois to record a conversation without both parties consenting, the city's official reaction was "we reminded employees to continue following the law" instead of prosecuting anyone. When asked about the illegal recordings, Mayor Rahm Emanuel brushed off the media's concerns, characterizing the issue as "much ado about nothing." He also justified his staff's actions by saying he should be able to have records of his office's interactions with others. For more details, see Robert Channick, "Emanuel: Taping of Reporters 'Much Ado About Nothing,'" *Chicago Tribune*, November 12, 2012, http://articles.chicagotribune.com/2012-11-12/news/ct-met-city-hall-recordings-1112-20121112_1_gerould-kern-consent-karen-flax.

5. *ACLU v. Alvarez*, 679 F.3d 583, 608 (7th Cir. 2012) (holding that a state "eavesdropping" ban, which prohibited audio records of on-duty police officers, restricted the "preservation and dissemination of information and ideas");

Glik v. Cunniffe, 655 F.3d 78 (1st Cir. 2011) (upholding a plaintiff's right to record police aggression during an arrest in a public forum); Statement of Interest of the United States, *Garcia v. Montgomery Cnty.*, No. 8:12-cv-03592 (D. Md. Mar. 4, 2013) (arguing that it is within an individual's First Amendment rights to record police activity in a public place).

6. *Glik v. Cunniffe* at 85–88 (ruling that the police's seizure of the plaintiff's video recording violated his Fourth Amendment rights because they had no probable cause to arrest him); *Johnson v. Hawe*, 388 F.3d 676, 685 (9th Cir. 2004) (holding that a police officer could not seize a bystander's video of him talking to other officers over a radio because such a seizure violated the bystander's Fourth Amendment rights).

7. See, e.g., Glenn Harlan Reynolds & John A. Steakley, "A Due Process Right to Record the Police," University of Tennessee Legal Studies Research Paper No. 190 (2012), available at http://papers.ssrn.com/sol3/papers. cfm?abstract_id=2043907 (arguing that there is a due process right to record law enforcement personnel in public and private settings in order to collect and preserve evidence).

8. See, e.g., *ACLU v. Alvarez*, 679 F.3d 583, 608 (7th Cir. 2012); *Glik v. Cunniffe*, 655 F.3d 78 (1st Cir. 2011); *Kelly v. Borough of Carlisle*, 622 F.3d 248, 258–59 (3d Cir. 2010); *Johnson v. Hawe*, 388 F.3d 676, 685 (9th Cir. 2004); *Smith v. City of Cumming*, 212 F.3d 1332, 1333 (11th Cir. 2000).

9. *ACLU v. Alvarez* at 594.

10. *Id.* at 595.

11. *Id.* at 597.

12. *Id.* at 606.

13. Richard A. Posner, *Sex and Reason* (1992).

14. *ACLU v. Alvarez* at 609 (Posner, J., dissenting).

15. *The Federalist* No. 48, at 311 (James Madison) (Clinton Rossiter ed., 1961).

16. *ACLU v. Alvarez* at 595 n.4.

17. *Id.* at 611 (Posner, J., dissenting).

18. *Id.* at 614 (Posner, J., dissenting) (recognizing that "[a]ccuracy is a social value" that public recording may promote "since a party to a conversation, including a police officer, may lie about what he heard or said").

19. Nina Golgowski, "Moment San Diego cop 'smashes man's phone and his face to the ground after he refused to stop recording,'" *Mail Online*, April 21, 2013, available at http://www.dailymail.co.uk/news/article-2312324/Moment-San-Diego-cop-smashes-mans-phone-face-ground-refuses-stop-recording.html#ixzz2S3UTi3YF.

20. *United States v. Virginia*, 518 U.S. 515, 533 (1996) (applying intermediate scrutiny in a case involving gender-based classification).

21. *Weinberger v. Wiesenfeld*, 420 U.S. 636, 648 (1975) (emphasis added). The idea that it is categorically impossible for courts to identify the government's actual ends is sufficiently widespread that it is worth emphasizing how utterly irreconcilable it is not only with common sense, but with longstanding Supreme Court doctrine as well: *Miller v. Johnson*, 515 U.S. 900, 912–20 (1995) ("Nor can the State's districting legislation be rescued by mere recitation of purported communities of interest. . . . It is apparent that it was not alleged shared interests but rather the object of maximizing the District's black population and obtaining Justice Department approval that in fact explained the General Assembly's actions."); *Church of the Lukumi Babalu Aye, Inc. v. City of Hialeah*, 508 U.S. 520, 540 (1993) (concluding that ordinances forbidding animal sacrifice "had as their object the suppression of religion" and observing that "as in equal protection cases, we may determine the city council's object from both direct and circumstantial evidence"); *Richmond v. J. A. Croson Co.*, 488 U.S. 469, 508 (1989) (determining that administrative convenience motivated the city of Richmond to establish a minority set-aside system and that that interest did not justify "a rigid line drawn on the basis of a suspect classification"); *Edwards v. Aguillard*, 482 U.S. 578, 586–87 (1987) ("While the Court is normally deferential to a State's articulation of a secular purpose, it is required that the statement of such purpose be sincere and not a sham."); *Hunter v. Underwood*, 471 U.S. 222, 231–32 (1985) (dismissing a state government's post hoc justifications for disenfranchisement laws because of overwhelming evidence of race-based legislative motivations; the Court was also unmoved by the state's other rationalization, that the law was intended to discriminate against both poor whites and blacks); *Mississippi Univ. for Women v. Hogan*, 458 U.S. 718, 729–30 (1982) (holding

that prohibiting male enrollment at a women's state school was not substantially related to combatting discrimination against women, but rather perpetuated the stereotype that only women could be nurses; the Court also noted that the state's policy of allowing men to audit classes at that school "fatally undermined" the state's argument that single-sex education was more beneficial for women); *Califano v. Goldfarb*, 430 U.S. 199, 216–17 (1977) (analyzing legislative history to determine that Congress's purposes in enforcing differential gender-based standards for receiving Social Security benefits was not remedial; instead, Congress made discriminatory assumptions that "[did] not suffice to justify a gender-based discrimination in the distribution of employment-related benefits"); *Eisenstadt v. Baird*, 405 U.S. 438, 443 (1972) (holding that the asserted moral purpose of a Massachusetts law banning distribution of contraceptives to unmarried people could not actually be the legislature's intent, and that the actual purpose, which was instead to limit contraception, was unconstitutional).

22. *Edenfield v. Fane*, 507 U.S. 761, 770 (1993).

23. *Ezell v. City of Chicago*, 651 F.3d 684, 709 (7th Cir. 2011).

24. *City of Los Angeles v. Alameda Books, Inc.*, 535 U.S. 425, 438 (2002) (plurality opinion).

25. *Id.*; see also *Edenfield v. Fane*, 507 U.S. 761, 770–71 (1993) (holding that "a governmental body seeking to sustain a restriction on commercial speech must demonstrate that the harms it recites are real and that its restrictions will in fact alleviate them to a material degree").

26. *McBurney v. Young*, 133 S. Ct. 1709, 1715 (2013).

27. *Toomer v. Witsell*, 384 U.S. 385, 395 (1948).

28. *McBurney v. Young* at 1715 (emphasis added).

29. 323 U.S. 214 (1944).

30. *Korematsu v. United States*, 584 F. Supp. 1406, 1422, 1424 app. (N.D. Cal. 1984). Attached to the decision as appendixes were Justice Department memos revealing that the government's arguments had been willfully inaccurate representations to the Supreme Court.

31. See, e.g., Kermit Roosevelt III, *The Myth of Judicial Activism: Making Sense of Supreme Court Decisions* 223–24 (2006) (citing several sources including

Justice Delayed: The Record of the Japanese American Internment Cases (Peter Irons ed., 1989)).

32. Fred Korematsu's conviction for violating the so-called exclusion order was vacated by a federal district court in 1984 after the government declined to defend its litigation misconduct before the Supreme Court four decades earlier. *Korematsu v. United States*, 584 F. Supp. 1406 (N.D. Cal. 1984). In 2011, the Justice Department released a statement, known as a "confession of error," acknowledging that it had withheld key facts from the courts that "undermined the rationale behind the internment" of Japanese Americans during World War II. Neal Katyal, "Confession of Error: The Solicitor General's Mistakes During the Japanese-American Internment Cases," U.S. Dep't of Justice, May 20, 2011, http://blogs.justice.gov/main/archives/1346.

33. Brad Heath & Kevin McCoy, "Prosecutors' Conduct Can Tip Justice Scales," *USA Today*, September 23, 2010, http://usatoday30.usatoday.com/news/washington/judicial/2010-09-22-federal-prosecutors-reform_N.htm.

34. *United States v. Childs*, 447 F.3d 541, 545 (7th Cir. 2006).

35. Michelle Alexander, "Why Police Lie Under Oath," *New York Times*, February 3, 2013, at SR4, available at http://www.nytimes.com/2013/02/03/opinion/sunday/why-police-officers-lie-under-oath.html?pagewanted=1&_r=5&.&.

36. *Hearing on the Nomination of John G. Roberts, Jr. to Be Chief Justice of the United States*, Hearing Before the Senate Committee on the Judiciary, September 12–15, 2005, 109th Cong., at 55 (statement of John G. Roberts, Jr.).

37. See, e.g., *Powers v. Harris*, 379 F.3d 1208, 1217 (10th Cir. 2004).

38. 508 U.S. 307 (1993).

39. *Beach Commc'ns, Inc. v. FCC*, 959 F.2d 975, 990 (D.C. Cir. 1992) (Mikva, C.J., concurring).

40. *Beach Commc'ns, Inc. v. FCC*, 965 F.2d 1103, 1105 (D.C. Cir. 1992), *rev'd sub nom. FCC v. Beach Commc'ns, Inc.*, 508 U.S. 307 (1993).

41. *FCC v. Beach Commc'ns, Inc. v. FCC*, 508 U.S. 307, 317–20 (1993); for an unofficial transcript of *FCC v. Beach Communications*, see http://www.oyez.org/cases/1990–1999/1992/1992_92_603; see also *Panama City Med. Diagnostic*

Ltd. v. Williams, 13 F.3d 1541, 1546 n.3 (noting that "one of the rationales relied on by the Court [in *Beach Communications*] was proffered not by the legislature in support of the challenged statute, but rather by a circuit judge, concurring in the circuit court's opinion").

42. *Armour v. City of Indianapolis*, 946 N.E. 553 (Ind. 2011), *aff'd*, 132 S. Ct. 2073 (2012).

43. *Armour v. City of Indianapolis*, 132 S. Ct. 2073, 2085 (2012) (Roberts, C.J., dissenting).

44. *Armour v. City of Indianapolis*, 946 N.E.2d 553, 562–63 (Ind. 2011), *aff'd*, 132 S. Ct. 2073 (2012) (emphasis added).

45. *Armour v. City of Indianapolis*, 132 S. Ct. 2073 (2012).

46. Randy E. Barnett, *Restoring the Lost Constitution: The Presumption of Liberty* 226 (2004).

47. *Sikes v. Teleline, Inc.*, 281 F.3d 1350, 1362 (11th Cir. 2002) (quoted in Timothy Sandefur, "In Defense of Substantive Due Process, or the Promise of Lawful Rule," 35 *Harv. J.L. & Pub. Pol'y* 284, 301 (2012)).

48. *Florida ex rel. Atty. Gen. v. Dep't of Health and Human Servs.*, 648 F.3d 1235, 1284 (11th Cir. 2011), *aff'd in part, rev'd in part sub nom. Nat'l Fed'n of Indep. Bus. v. Sebelius*, 132 S. Ct. 2566 (2012).

49. For a list of cases, see note 16 in Chapter 2.

50. *Craigmiles v. Giles*, 312 F.3d 220, 223–24 (6th Cir. 2002).

51. *Id.* at 225 (internal quotation and citations omitted).

52. *St. Joseph Abbey v. Castille*, 712 F.3d 215 (5th Cir. 2013).

53. *Id.* at 218.

54. *Id.* at 226.

55. *Id.*

56. *Id.* at 227.

57. 379 F.3d 1208 (10th Cir. 2004).

58. *Powers v. Harris*, 379 F.3d 1208, 1217 (10th Cir. 2004) (internal quotation and citation omitted).

59. *Id.* at 1221–22.

60. *Merrifield v. Lockyer*, 547 F.3d 978 (9th Cir. 2008).

Chapter 9: From Abdication to Engagement

1. Richard A. Epstein, *How Progressives Rewrote the Constitution* 83 (2006).

2. See, e.g., Jeffrey M. Jones, "Americans Divided on Repeal of 2010 Healthcare Law," *Gallup Politics*, February 27, 2012, available at http://www.gallup.com/poll/152969/Americans-Divided-Repeal-2010-Healthcare-Law.aspx (reporting Gallup's finding that 72 percent of people polled believed Obamacare was unconstitutional).

3. See, e.g., *Hearing on the Nomination of John G. Roberts, Jr. to Be Chief Justice of the United States*, Hearing Before the Senate Committee on the Judiciary, September 12–15, 2005, 109th Cong., at 150, 152–53, 169–70 (statements of John G. Roberts, Jr.). When asked to discuss particular cases and legal situations, Chief Justice Roberts often made statements such as "I don't want to answer a particular hypothetical that could come before the Court," and "I'm cautious, of course, about expressing an opinion on a matter that might come before the Court." See also *The Nomination of Elena Kagan to Be an Associate Justice of the Supreme Court of the United States*, Hearing Before the Senate Committee on the Judiciary, June 28–July 1, 2010, 111th Cong., at 80. Elena Kagan, now an associate justice, demurred from answering certain questions on the grounds that "it [is] inappropriate for a nominee to ever give any indication of how she would rule in a case that would come before the Court. And . . . it would be inappropriate to do so in a somewhat veiled manner by essentially grading cases." She instead invited senators to ask questions about her approach to statutory interpretation and her judicial philosophy.

4. 410 U.S. 113 (1973).

5. 262 U.S. 390 (1923).

6. 268 U.S. 510 (1925).

7. *Meyer v. Nebraska*, 262 U.S. 390, 401 (1923).

8. *Pierce v. Soc'y of Sisters*, 268 U.S. 510, 534–35 (1925).

9. *Meyer v. Nebraska* at 401–02 (quoting Plato's *Republic*).

10. Randy E. Barnett, *Restoring the Lost Constitution: The Presumption of Liberty* 234 & n.42 (2004) (documenting Judge Bork's application of the ink-blot

metaphor to the Ninth Amendment and the privileges or immunities clause of the Fourteenth Amendment).

11. *Zablocki v. Redhail*, 434 U.S. 374, 383 (1978) (confirming that the right to marry "is of fundamental importance"); *Turner v. Safley*, 482 U.S. 72, 95 (1987) (holding that the constitutional right to marry applies even to prison inmates).

12. *United States v. Guest*, 383 U.S. 745, 757 (1966) (explaining that "[t]he constitutional right to travel from one State to another, and necessarily to use the highways and other instrumentalities of interstate commerce in doing so, occupies a position fundamental to the concept of our Federal Union. It is a right that has been firmly established and repeatedly recognized."); *Shapiro v. Thompson*, 394 U.S. 618, 629–30 (1969).

13. *Moore v. City of E. Cleveland*, 431 U.S. 494, 499–500, 506 (1977).

14. *Skinner v. Oklahoma*, 316 U.S. 535, 541–42 (1942).

15. *District of Columbia v. Heller*, 554 U.S. 570, 599 (2008).

16. *Ross v. United States*, 910 F.2d 1422, 1424–25 (7th Cir. 1990).

17. *Roe v. Wade*, 410 U.S. 113, 173 (1973) (Rehnquist, J., dissenting); see also *Doe v. Bolton*, 410 U.S. 179, 222–23 (1973) (White and Rehnquist, JJ., dissenting in companion case to *Roe*) (emphasizing that the case did not involve, and the Court had no cause to consider, application of Georgia law to "those pregnancies posing substantial hazards to either life or health").

18. See, e.g., Robert H. Bork, *The Tempting of America: The Political Seduction of the Law* 32 (1990).

19. *Id. Dred Scott v. Sandford*, 60 U.S. (19 How) 393 (1857) is the infamous case in which the Supreme Court held that people of African descent could never be American citizens and argued, in dictum, that the federal government had no authority to outlaw slavery in the territories because doing so would violate the property rights of slave owners.

20. Jeffrey Rosen, "Going Rogue," *New Republic*, April 2011, at 12, available at http://www.newrepublic.com/article/politics/magazine/85326/health-care-lawsuits-interstate-commerce-personal-liberty.

21. J. Harvie Wilkinson III, *Cosmic Constitutional Theory: Why Americans Are Losing Their Inalienable Right to Self-Governance* 9 (2012).

22. *Id.* at 114.

23. Stephen Breyer, *Active Liberty: Interpreting Our Democratic Constitution* 4 (2005).

24. *Id.* at 14.

25. 274 U.S. 200, 207 (1927).

26. *Powers v. Harris*, 379 F.3d 1208, 1221 (10th Cir. 2004).

27. Wilkinson, *Cosmic Constitutional Theory* at 106; see also *id.* at 20 & n.47 (citing Antonin Scalia, "Common-Law Courts in a Civil-Law System: The Role of United States Federal Courts in Interpreting the Constitution and Laws," in Antonin Scalia, *A Matter of Interpretation: Federal Courts and the Law* 3, 40 (Amy Gutmann ed., 1997)).

28. See, e.g., Kermit Roosevelt III, "Constitutional Calcification: How the Law Becomes What the Court Does," 91 *Va. L. Rev.* 1649, 1661–62 (2005). See also Clint Bolick, *David's Hammer: The Case for an Activist Judiciary* 160–61 (2007) (asserting that while "[s]ome would argue that . . . it is dangerous to entrust judges with power they can so recklessly exercise," restoring checks and balances would prevent gross abuses of power); Barnett, *Restoring the Lost Constitution* at 266–67 ("Some may object that a Presumption of Liberty would place altogether too much power in judges. A reliance on judges, however, is unavoidable in a constitutional system in which only courts are available to stand between individual citizens and majority and minority factions operating through representative government.").

29. See Elizabeth Price Foley, *Liberty for All: Reclaiming Individual Privacy in a New Era of Public Morality* 135 (2006).

30. 316 U.S. 535 (1942).

31. *Clayton v. Steinagel*, 885 F. Supp. 2d 1212, 1215–16 (D. Utah 2012); *Cornwell v. Hamilton*, 80 F. Supp. 2d 1101, 1107–08 (S.D. Cal. 1999).

32. Institute for Justice Litigation Backgrounder, "Brushing Out Utah's African Hairbraiding Laws," http://www.ij.org/utah-hairbraiding-background.

33.   *Clayton v. Steinagel*; *Cornwell v. Hamilton* (same in California); *Uqdah v. District of Columbia*, 785 F. Supp. 1015 (D.D.C. 1992), *vacated as moot sub nom. Uqdah v. D.C. Bd. of Cosmetology*, 1993 U.S. App. LEXIS 14569 (D.C. Cir. Apr. 30, 1993) (upholding Washington D.C.'s requirement that hair braiders become licensed cosmetologists).

Index